LOUISIANA STATE UNIVERSITY STUDIES

Max Goodrich, General Editor

Humanities Series

Donald E. Stanford, Editor

Number Sixteen

Dryden: A Study in Heroic Characterization

DRYDEN
A Study
in Heroic Characterization

~·~·~·~·~

by
Selma Assir Zebouni

Louisiana State University Press
BATON ROUGE
MCMLXV

To Suzanne

PREFACE

SINCE IT CONCENTRATES on form, sources, and influences, a large part
of the modern criticism on Dryden's heroic plays neglects characterization when it does not ignore it altogether. One of the major consequences of such a neglect is to foster the image of the "heroic"
hero as a self-centered individual whose superhuman valor is directed toward the achievement of both a limitless personal desire
for power and a superhuman love for a perfect heroine. A wide-
spread assumption that the heroic tragedy is essentially a "romantic"
manifestation derives directly from such a view of the hero. A parallel assumption is that the heroic tragedy is a genre alien to the
English genius and outside the normal evolution of the English
drama. A more or less strict adherence to neoclassical rules derived
from continental and mainly French critics is made partly responsible for the failure of the English heroic tragedy.

This book re-evaluates some of the above-mentioned critical arguments, through a study of the characterization of the hero in
Dryden's heroic tragedy. The hero is studied in relation to the plot
situation—that is, the play considered as drama and not as a rostrum
for the voicing of various ideas—and an interpretation of the arche-
type of the heroic hero is offered. This interpretation contradicts
the commonly accepted one and shows him instead as the embodiment of common sense and order. With this view of the hero in
mind, Dryden's heroic tragedies are then analyzed in relation to
the contemporary intellectual and historical milieu and to Dryden's
own psychological evolution. As a corollary object of interest, the
hero in some of Dryden's other serious plots is compared to the

hero of the heroic plays. It has also seemed of value to compare plays by Dryden, Corneille, and Racine and to show the affinity between Dryden's and Corneille's work as opposed to Racine's.

The conclusion arrived at in this study is that Dryden's heroic plays—far from being a "passing whim," a movement outside the main course of English literature—are on the contrary a true reflection of the period and of the author and an important link in the evolution of English drama.

For his encouragement and kindness during and after the elaboration of this work, I owe an immense debt of gratitude to Professor W. J. Olive of the English department of Louisiana State University.

S. A. Z.

CONTENTS

DRYDEN: A Study in Heroic Characterization

CHAPTER 1

CONTEMPORARY TRENDS
IN DRYDEN CRITICISM

CRITICISM OF THE Restoration heroic tragedy, though extensive, has not yet arrived at a detailed and comprehensive characterization of the hero. Commentaries, remarks, even interpretations are numerous, but are to be found only in connection with other problems. In many instances, this lack of interest in the psychology of the hero results from the opinion that there is no psychology to speak of. Lewis N. Chase calls this psychology "impossible because beyond nature. . . . There was little or no attempt to draw men and women, but rather to present abstract human qualities. . . . The Restoration hero and his train proved to be made of such perishable stuff because the composition was found wanting in that sense, which to the exaltation of the populace they despised, is called common sense." [1] J. W. Tupper considers characterization in the heroic play "very slight" because "no attempt is made to build plot about character . . . plot consists of a series of happenings more or less theatric in nature, and without any vital connection with each other, and with the character figuring in them . . . the characterization of these plays amounts to nothing. . . ." [2] Margaret Sherwood holds the opinion that "there are no subtle strokes in character treatment." [3] B. J. Pendlebury concludes that "Dryden can hardly be praised for the psychological truth of his character-drawing." [4] Allardyce Nicoll speaks of the "impossible psychology" of the heroic tragedy. [5] Bonamy Dobrée thought no differently in 1956 than he did in 1929,

3

when he said, "Absence of subtlety, or, in the modern jargon, a lack of psychology, is what they [the heroic tragedies] can most justly be reproached with." [6]

The list of critics holding these same opinions is by no means exhausted. But granting that Dryden is not a profound psychologist, yet we are confronted in each of his plays with at least one character who speaks and acts for five acts; something can and should be done to analyze him; the apparent lack of profundity of the character is no excuse for brushing the problem aside. It is good at this point to refrain from citing Dryden's opinion concerning the importance of the hero since his practice could be a far cry from his theory. This is what Chase seems to imply:

> . . . character was doubtless considered an important part of dramatic construction. . . . The name in itself—heroic drama—implies necessarily the presence and infers the importance of a hero. To portray him as the word was understood in dramatic parlance of that time, must have been a primary object. . . . It is plain that if this was the theory, practice did not bear it out. It is also plain that whatever the theory, practice did not bear it out for the ideal lacked consistency.[7]

Yet more often than not, the same critics who have nothing but contempt for the characterization of the hero are careful to point out its importance. Chase's conclusion is that the heroic tragedy "presented a shadow, at least, of true heroic character." [8] Moreover, "the reader's impressions of the plays are usually dominated by the figure of the hero," says Pendlebury, who attributes the "predominance of the hero" to the influence of epic poetry.[9]

This failure to try to understand the psychology of the hero in the heroic tragedy would be negligible if it were not that it distorts the critics' final judgment of the heroic tragedy itself. Having to account for a literary phenomenon which occupied at least one generation of writers [10] (and among them the acknowledged foremost writer of his age—Dryden), ultimately they almost all do one of two things: blame what they call the deficiencies of the heroic play on continental and mainly French influence; or, on the contrary, minimize these influences and try very hard to make heroic tragedy fit into a preceding English dramatic genre, calling it a degeneracy of that genre. Both schools of critics more often than not end up by concentrating on the sources of the heroic tragedy rather than on the heroic tragedy proper. When not occupied with the sources, they turn to questions of form. In examining some of this criticism, the chronological approach is probably the most rewarding since it shows better than any other the interplay and exchange of ideas among critics.

Starting with Sir Walter Scott, we find that for him "the heroic, or rhyming plays were borrowed from the French, to whose genius they are better suited than to the British . . . we have little doubt that the heroic tragedies were the legitimate offspring of the French Romances of Calprenède and Scudéry." [11] Scott is not alone in his opinion: "The heroic plays," says A. W. Ward, "from the first stood under the direct influence of foreign literary growths." [12] Chase agrees that "the French form of tragedy was welcomed in England, with rhyme, but without reason; and though it soon drifted away in spirit from its origin, it remained to the end foreign, exotic, un-English." [13] Though we are able to follow Chase's general trend of thought, we cannot do more since he fails to show how and why the heroic tragedy "drifted away in spirit from its origin," and does not give a definition of what is "un-English."

Though concurring in the idea of French influence, C. G. Child takes the other point of view: "Dryden followed Davenant in his use of his sources [the French romances], as he did in the manner of his treatment of the material thus drawn." [14] Child considers this important because otherwise "a further point of paramount importance will not clearly appear—the development of the heroic play out of the earlier Romantic drama," since in Davenant "the process of perversion of Fletcherian romanticism can be distinctly traced." [15]

Tupper elaborates on Child's premises: "It is, however, with the romantic plays of Beaumont and Fletcher that the most striking resemblances will be found to exist." He does, however, make a distinction which could be fruitful: "It is the removal of an external obstacle and not internal conflict, that here [in the heroic play] contributes action. . . ." [16] Unfortunately, he does not develop this idea.

Margaret Sherwood tends to agree with the theory of foreign influence: "The Heroic plays have certain importance from the fact that they form a curious commentary on Restoration taste, but they hardly form a link in the development of English drama. They reflect only a passing whim." [17]

F. E. Schelling is a staunch advocate of the Beaumont and Fletcher influence theory: "For in this justly famous tragicomedy [*Philaster*] combine all the qualities of the species to set a standard from which this type of play was little to vary until it declined into its logical successor, the Restoration heroic drama." [18] Comparing both types of plays, he comes to the conclusion that "when everything has been said, all that the authors of the new heroic play accomplished by way of actual novelty was to exaggerate what had already been exaggerated, to heighten still more and make more florid an already exalted diction, and to substitute for the supple blank-verse of Fletcher or the hybrid prose-verse of Carlell, the regular tread of the rhymed couplet." [19]

Pendlebury disagrees strongly, minimizing both the national and French influence and emphasizing instead the influence of epic form: "These views seem to me to exaggerate the influence of Beaumont and Fletcher on the heroic drama, and to ignore the essential quality which distinguishes the Restoration heroic play from their tragicomedy. It is quite easy to prove that the heroic play has much in common with the decadent romantic drama, but it is the imposition of epic form on the romantic material which creates the heroic play." [20] He then proceeds to point out the differences between the two types of plays, and one has the impression he is going to consider the problem of character. "It [Dryden's drama] limited the heroic play to a code of sentiment, and it produced a unity which was rather epic than dramatic, since it depended on the character of the hero." [21] But after emphasizing Dryden's lack of psychological insight, he loses himself in the question of form: "Since then the most striking characteristics of the heroic play, the epic construction, the unity of tone, and the predominance of the hero, cannot be regarded as being inherited from Beaumont and Fletcher, it is obvious that their origins must be sought in that critical theory [*i.e.*, epic influence]. . . ." [22]

Allardyce Nicoll's criticism of the heroic tragedy is mainly descriptive: "The heroic play as well as the comedy of manners is to be explained by a three-fold formula—Elizabethan sub-stratum, the spirit of the age and foreign influence." [23] On the whole, Nicoll's treatment is confined to examination of these sources.

W. S. Clark goes back to Scott's stand: "The heroic plays mark a distinct breach with the past." [24] In his opinion the "foundation" and "inspiration" of the heroic play are the French romances.

Bonamy Dobrée studies the heroic tragedy from the point of view of form. "The dramatists of the day were trying to express romantic ideas in a form specially evolved for the classical." [25] He explains the heroic tragedy by the need which the age had for heroism. "The aspect which first strikes every reader of Restoration tragedy is its unreality. . . . The age was hungry for heroism, and feeling itself balked of it in real life was happy to find it in its art." [26] Allardyce Nicoll has arrived at the same conclusion: "The age was debilitated; it was distinctly unheroic; and yet it was not so cynical as to throw over entirely the inculcation of heroism. . . . The heroic play is like a tale of a Land of No-Where. . . . We are interested in that land, but we do not hope ever to enter therein. The persons who move and speak there are not our equals, nor do they even draw the same breath as we do." [27] In his 1956 study on Dryden, Dobrée again expresses the same view and calls the heroic tragedy "glorious extravaganza. . . . Emotions, states of mind, which are to the final degree romantic, are tailored into, or at least partly wear, severe classical garb. . . . Be prepared to enter a world of absolute emotions. . . ." [28]

Kathleen Lynch, disagreeing with Clark (and Scott), holds that the French romances throw little light on the structure of heroic drama, and though she admits some influence derived from Marlowe and Beaumont and Fletcher, she argues, nevertheless, that the "marked Platonism" of the heroic drama differentiates it from their dramatic work: "Fletcher's lovers are not, however, Platonic ritualists. They do not pass through the successful stages of discipline in love whereby the personages of heroic drama are tested as love's converts." [29] However, she arrives at her conclusion in a somewhat puzzling way: she notes that though Dryden took many of his plots from the French romances, "the play remains widely separated from the romances in method and effect"; she points out that Dryden omitted "the charming girlhood of Almahide, the sedate descriptions of Moorish revels," when he wrote *The Conquest of Granada*. (Considering that he still wrote ten acts, many readers are probably grateful for the omission.) "His chief concern is with the events of the ninth and shortest book of the romance and these events he amplifies and reshapes in dramatic form, placing emphasis on moments which are of high interest from the dramatist's point of view. In thus selecting from the formless French romances suitable ingredients for Platonic drama, Dryden must have been influenced by the Platonic dramatists." [30]

The essential weakness of this argument is pointed out by S. C. Osborn, who reveals Miss Lynch's own admission that "in Dryden's plays Platonic interests are at times overshadowed by claims of patriotism, personal honor, and filial devotion." [31] Osborn refutes the point that these plays are studies in Platonic love: "Unquestionably Dryden's heroic love does reflect the sentimental, metaphysical Platonism of French heroic romances and drama," but he contends that "Dryden's drama contains not one but two kinds of love, each of a long tradition. . . ." [32] He goes on to analyze the concept of "heroical love" in Robert Burton's *Anatomy of Melancholy* and states that "Dryden's plays . . . exhibit all of the conditions, symptoms and effects of heroical love. . . . Dryden's characters almost invariably describe love as a physical and mental disease. . . . In each play erotic passion and jealousy provide nearly all the motivation." [33] Osborn's criticism is interesting; unfortunately he never relates the characters' utterances to the plot situation, nor does he discriminate as to who says what and when. Moreover, he offers such sweeping statements as, ". . . no heroic lover is expected to behave rationally." [34]

Emphasizing the influence of contemporary philosophical ideas, Mildred Hartsock displays the same shortcoming. Having arrived at the conclusion that Dryden was very much under the influence of Hobbesian ideology, she attempts "to study important intellectual trends of the 17th Century which are reflected in the plays of Dryden; to discover in which of these the poet was most apparently interested; and finally, through comparison of the serious and comic plays and through reference to the non-dramatic work, to secure what evidence there is of the writer's own probable belief." [35] Here again the critic analyzes speeches, cites out of context, and arrives at unwarranted conclusions since she does not discriminate between villain and hero and does not take into account the plot situation. For instance, when she states that "Dryden's characters are self-centered and their conceptions of the virtue are selfishly utilitarian," all her examples are drawn from characterizations of villains, except for one speech of Aureng-Zebe's which she cites out of context.[36] We shall have occasion later in this study to show how, on the contrary, this same speech viewed in relation to the rest of the play makes the hero even more unselfishly heroic. Her conclusion is that Dryden's plays "show no significant concern with the more idealistic current. . . . The prevailing spirit is worldly, skeptical, even materialistic." [37] She may be right for the particular passage she is considering, but it is certainly not warranted as a general conclusion, since it is not Dryden who is speaking but a character in a play. The distinction as to whether a hero or a villain is made to be the exponent of Hobbesian ideas makes all the difference in the world, since we are to admire and imitate the hero, and rejoice in the villain's downfall.

This influence of Hobbesian ideas is rejected by J. A. Winterbottom. He cites examples from heroic plays in which reason is not just a means to satisfy the passions as in Hobbes and draws attention to the many instances of moral obligations which the heroes obey unselfishly.[38] Unfortunately his study is not exhaustive and is simply meant to point to some of the inconsistencies of Mildred Hartsock's article.

A. E. Parsons, like Pendlebury, goes back to the theory of epic influence and holds that the heroic play was "produced by the shaping of romantic material to the epic pattern."[39] His approach is new, however, in that he finds two currents into which heroic theory developed and which he calls Homeric and Virgilian, the Homeric type being exemplified in the French drama (more "masculine") and the Virgilian in the English drama "which centers in the union of a pair of lovers. . . ."[40]

Cecil V. Deane in his *Dramatic Theory and the Rhymed Heroic Play* concentrates mainly on questions of form and sources,[41] whereas D. N. Smith has nothing essential to say on the characterization in the heroic plays, but nevertheless uses such words as "extravagance" and "bravura" in speaking of them.[42]

A more recent article by Thomas H. Fujimura is rather interesting in that it tries to show the heroic tragedy as an expression of the age, conveying some of the ideas, ideals, and tendencies of that age. He disagrees entirely with the opinion of Nicoll, Dobrée, and Chase that the Restoration public, being unheroic, found a vicarious satisfaction in heroic plays. "Actually, there is little evidence for the common assumption that the Restoration was unheroic, and that consequently the age was hungry for heroism. Further, no one familiar with its youthful vigor, its vital interest in science, and its optimistic confidence in the powers of reason and its empiricism, would regard the period as debilitated."[43] He contends that critics have overlooked the intellectual appeal of Dryden's plays: "It would not be surprising to find a skeptical and naturalistically inclined audience patronizing his plays if these qualities are conspicuous in them."[44] Though agreeing with Mildred Hartsock as to the abundance of Hobbesian elements in Dryden's plays, he points out that her conclusions are unwarranted. He is of the opinion that the central theme of these plays is the struggle between love and honor, two seemingly idealistic conceptions, but his contention is that

> . . . even the central theme, the struggle between love and honor, is strongly naturalistic in conception. . . . These two concepts must be regarded primarily as naturalistic notions; that is, they represent neither a spiritual nor a moral ideal but rather a passional commitment to sex and self-aggrandizement. . . . This picture of man represents, in essence, the naturalistic subversion of Christian humanism, which emphasizes man's rationality and his control of the passions. . . . Dryden's heroic plays then extol the primacy of passion, and sex is glorified as the most powerful of human passions." [45]

Fujimura transforms honor into a naturalistic concept by having it replace reason and making of it a passion: "Honor for the naturalistic opponents of the Christian humanists [is] . . . the ireful virtue. [It] . . . is nothing more or less than one of the dominant passions. . . ." [46] And he qualifies the intellectual appeal that Dryden's plays had on their audiences as "cultural primitivism": it is "Dryden's primitivism" that appeals to the "sophisticated Restoration audience." [47]

The weaknesses of Fujimura's conclusions are brought out by Jean Gagen, who ably points out that one can find in Dryden's plays many aspects of one concept, including those that flaunt all moral laws and represent a passion of commitment to sex and self-aggrandizement; but that "the heroes and heroines . . . are committed to concepts of love and honor which have a real, though romantically exaggerated, ethical content." [48] She notes that Fujimura disregarded Osborn's conclusions as to the two kinds of love found in Dryden's heroic tragedies, and she proceeds to a discussion of the concept of honor. Basing this discussion on Curtis Watson's *Shakespeare and the Renaissance Concept of Honor,*[49] she comes to the conclusion that "the view of love and honor as primarily naturalistic passions devoid of ethical considerations is characteristic of only the most deeply-dyed villains in Dryden's heroic plays. . . . Repudiations of love and honor as ethical ideals are never permanently sanctioned by the heroes and heroines of these plays." [50]

A recent article of Cyrus Hoy does not change this general picture of the criticism of the heroic tragedy. He finds that tragedy "comes to dwell more and more exclusively on erotic passion as its one and only theme. . . . The tragic issue comes typically to turn upon a more or less abstractly conceived conflict of reason and passion. . . ." [51] Relying on Aristotle's definition of tragedy, he contends that Restoration tragedy is not tragic since the virtuous do not suffer, but is "idealistic and sentimental, which at first glance seems odd, given the naturalistic, materialistic, scientific bent of Restoration thought." [52] His explanation is nothing but a reshaping of what Nicoll, Chase, and Dobrée have said before: "All of which [ideals of love, honor, reason, virtue] are proportionately appealing as they are remote from the experience of the times." [53] He seems, however, to contradict himself when he goes on to say: "In Restoration London, love means sex, honor is a word, reason is the shrewdest calculating self-interest, virtue is a sham. . . . As has often been pointed out, there is a sense in which Restoration comedy and tragedy balance and complement one another, with the comedy portraying things as they are, and the tragedy portraying things as they might be or ought to be." [54] He concludes that "Restoration tragedy is 'theatrical' in the worst sense: that is to say, the sense in which drama falsifies life in order to project onto the stage the collective image of itself which the audience wishes to see." [55]

Though by no means exhaustive, this review of the criticism of Dryden's heroic tragedies is lengthy enough to show a general lack of concern with Dryden's characterization. The plays are mainly studied from the point of view of sources and influences, form, or ideas and concepts embodied in them. When a character is analyzed, the analysis is only an illustration in a discussion about an idea or concept.

The object of this study is not primarily to refute any of the above-cited opinions. It is rather to approach the problem of Dryden's plays from a different point of view, from the inside rather than from the outside, and to use the hero as the means to this approach. It is hoped that through a study of the characterization of the hero and his relation to the plot, a more sympathetic if not better understanding of the heroic play will be gained; and mainly, the understanding that the heroic play is not just a "passing whim" but an integral part of the neoclassical period which it reflects and embodies.

CHAPTER 2

THE HERO
IN DRYDEN'S HEROIC PLAYS

CRITICS SEEM TO agree as to which of Dryden's plays are essentially "heroic"; they implicitly limit his plays in this genre to *The Indian Queen* (1665), *The Indian Emperor* (1667), *Tyrannic Love* (1670), *The Conquest of Granada* (1672), and *Aureng-Zebe* (1676). George Saintsbury, for instance, says: "*The Indian Emperor, Tyrannic Love,* and *The Two Conquests of Granada* form—*Aureng-Zebe,* though strictly speaking a 'heroic' play, is apart from and above the kind— the main body of Dryden's contribution to that kind itself." [1] *All for Love* is considered to be a break away from the "heroic" play; and it is implied that after 1676 Dryden did not write heroic plays.

Inasmuch as a thorough acquaintance with the plays is necessary to an understanding of the hero, and in view of the fact that these plays are so packed with action that it is difficult to remember them accurately, a brief summary of the main psychological traits of the most important characters is presented in the following pages.

In *The Indian Queen* the hero is undoubtedly Montezuma. He is valorous but rash and proud; a low passion like anger can make him forget his duty to his prince and to his love. He is perfectly aware of these duties and does not question them, but his passions can overcome his reason and make him act rashly; he needs Acacis to check him and direct him. Yet, though swayed by passion, Montezuma is a noble character because he is aware of what honor requires him to do and because eventually he surmounts his passions and acts rightly. Guided by reason he follows the right path.

Acacis is a perfect character, the embodiment of honor itself; he always knows which obligation comes first and is so much in control of his passions that for him there is never a hard choice to make. In turn, he serves his friend, his love, and his country whenever required. If what he does is hard for him to do, it is never apparent, and he is always unmistakably right because always "cool" and guided by reason. He is the ideal which Montezuma eventually attains through struggle against his passions.

Zempoalla, prey to her passions, cannot dominate them; her reason is of no help to her. She has no concept of the meaning of honor and can feel only low physical love as opposed to the spiritual elevating kind. The implication seems to be that when reason does not control the passions, these can only make a person low and base. The path to honor is through reason.

In *The Indian Emperor* it is rather difficult to pinpoint the hero. Though the play is named for Montezuma, he is certainly no more the hero than Zempoalla was the heroine in *The Indian Queen*. Montezuma is portrayed as an essentially noble man who has become base and pitiable through his abject love of Almeria; his is not a noble love, since his reason tells him he should fight it, and he cannot. He does not eventually overcome his weakness or vice and does not grow into a better man; he certainly is not a hero, because he remains a slave to his passions. Furthermore, his part is rather short, both in number of lines and in the part he takes in the action.

Both Guyomar and Cortez could be heroes. They win the battles they fight, and they both have undoubtedly noble natures, but with a difference. Cortez is brave in battle, fearless of death. He knows his duty to his king (he must conquer the Mexicans in spite of Cydaria), to his love (Almeria cannot make him forget Cydaria), to friendship (he frees Guyomar whenever he can), to honor (he will not take advantage of Orbellan). Like all noble natures he is extremely generous to friend and foe alike. The one flaw in his behavior is his submission to Cydaria's prayers and his promise to stop the fight for twenty-four hours, in spite of what he owes to his king. For a few moments he abandons himself to love rather than follow the dicta of honor: "Honor be gone, what art thou but a breath." However, fortune is kind to him for his men are already fighting, and he cannot stop them.

As to Guyomar, he is faultless; not one blemish can be detected in him. Though brave, he is never rash; though a lover, he is never subject to his passion. His essential characteristic is that he always knows what he is supposed to do according to the laws of honor—and does it. The one time he seems to hesitate as to what course to take, he does not hesitate for long: though Cortez is enemy to his country, he cannot let him be murdered. When he has to save either his father or his lover, he saves his father. He captures Cortez, but will not allow him to be mistreated and appoints himself his protector. When asked by Alibech to beg for Cortez's leniency, he is outraged and would rather lose his love than act basely: he will not save his country at the price of honor. If Cortez is the hero of the play, Guyomar is the perfect heroic hero. Always in control of his passions, his reason is his guide to true honor.

Odmar is an interesting character. There is not much at the start to distinguish him from Guyomar, and he is the first to deplore his father's enslavement by Almeria. His love for Alibech seems to be as noble and as respectful as Guyomar's and probably is. His first sign of weakness is when he chooses to save his love Alibech rather than his father. We know then that he is more subject to his passions than Guyomar. He himself admits there is nothing he can do to check his love. Everything was under control as long as he hoped to obtain Alibech; he even stops his father from killing Guyomar. But when he loses Alibech, he abandons himself entirely to his passions—not only to love, but to anger and desire for revenge—and he becomes a traitor to his country. Significantly, the quality of his love for Alibech changes; it immediately takes a physical turn and no longer prompts him to glorious deeds of war and valor. He cares for nothing but the physical possession of Alibech and is about to rape her when she is saved by the Spaniards. Furthermore, he is perfectly conscious of his own degradation: "Virtue, ill treated, from my soul is fled." When passion and not reason is in complete possession of the field, there is no sense of honor left.

What tilts the scales in favor of Guyomar for hero is the personality of Alibech, his lover. Cydaria is the weaker soul and does little more than whimper during the whole play. But Alibech has the soul of a heroine: she will control her love and give herself to whoever will serve his country best, which is no less than what Guyomar does. When she urges him to ask leniency from Cortez, it is still of her country that she is thinking; in her soul she knows he is right. Also, rather than betray her love, she chooses to die.

Almeria is a slave to her passions: revenge for her mother, pride in her beauty, lust for Cortez; whenever she acts, she acts basely.

Though she is as patriotic as Alibech, her means of winning is to have Cortez murdered. She is such a slave to her love that she can only bring destruction to herself. Her only moment of grandeur is when she surmounts her jealousy, and dying, unites Cydaria and Cortez. Once passions are under control, a character acts according to honor.

In *Tyrannic Love* the question has also been raised as to who is the hero of the play. Maximin has a rather large part, and his actions contribute to the progress of the plot. We are told he is, or rather has been, brave in battle, but he does not actually fight and win a battle during the course of the play. The main feature of this character is that he is a slave to his passions: lustful love, wild anger, cruelty, and pride. His ranting is nothing else than the expression of his surrender to his passions. His actions can only bring about his own doom. Having none of the "heroical" virtues, Maximin cannot be the hero. We can arrive at this conclusion even without Dryden's assurances: "The part of Maximin, against which these holy Criticks so much declaim, was designed by me to set off the Character of St. Catherine. . . . Have I proposed him as a pattern to be imitated, whom even for his impiety to his false Gods, I have so severely punish'd?" [2]

Neither is St. Catherine the heroine of the play: her part is very short, and she does practically nothing to advance the plot. She is a saint; her business is with heaven, not with earth, and she makes this clear to Berenice and Porphyrius; her terms are not theirs. Actually the "heroical" thing for her to do would be to renounce her "crown of martyrdom" in order to save Berenice's life. The only interesting trait about her is that she converts people through discussion, convincing them, by means of reason, of their errors.

The real "heroic" plot is the Berenice-Porphyrius plot rather than the Maximin–St. Catherine plot. Porphyrius, right from the start, is presented as a hero—a brave leader of men whom victory accompanies wherever he goes. He is aware of the multiple duties imposed on him by honor: duty to his emperor, to his love, to those who have won his gratitude (Valeria, for instance). His duty to his emperor is complicated by the fact that that emperor is a bloody tyrant. Even so, he rebels against him only after having severed all ties with him and because of a greater duty, that of saving the unjustly condemned Berenice from death. Whatever his actions, he never thinks of himself but only of others. He asks Berenice to reward his love only once and is quickly convinced of his error. In spite of Maximin's actions, it takes Porphyrius a long time to revolt, and his anger then is only a rightful one. He is a man who controls his passions; he consequently always acts according to the laws of honor.

Except for a small scene of jealousy, Berenice is the absolute pattern of virtue, reason, and honor. She loves Porphyrius and loathes Maximin, but being Maximin's wife she will act her part as best she can whether he wants it or not, and to protect Maximin she even does her best to get Porphyrius killed. She is Porphyrius' conscience, and if he gives signs of relenting, she is there to remind him of his duties, for which he is very grateful.

Valeria is a generous and noble soul. Her one flaw is her passion for Porphyrius. Though her passion is noble and makes her accomplish generous things, it is still a flaw because it is overwhelming: since Porphyrius does not love her, she should control her passion for him; she does not do so and is destroyed by its excess.

The hero of *The Conquest of Granada* (Part One) is, of course, Almanzor. He is extremely brave and apparently very strong; he scorns death as all brave men do; he is extremely proud and considers himself the subject of no one. Undoubtedly a very passionate man, his first action—helping the Abencerrages—is one of impulse even if the motive is noble: because theirs is the weaker side, his generosity prompts him to help them regardless of whether their cause is right or wrong. He cannot bear the Duke of Arcos' scorn and decides to set him free in order to vanquish him again. He is the prey of anger when Boabdelin refuses him the Duke. When Abdalla asks for his help, he does not take into consideration the rightfulness of Abdalla's claim and will help him merely out of friendship. He tries to resist his love for Almahide but cannot. When refused Almahide by Abdalla, he does not try to understand Abdalla's reasons but turns against him. Having freed Almahide, he obeys his passion to the point of insisting that she take him instead of Boabdelin. He relents only when she shows him the way to win her: by gaining her father's consent. Finally, he would rather die than give up Almahide.

That Almanzor's nature is noble is unquestioned. But he is also too much a prey to his passions. They make him behave rashly, and he fails to act perfectly in accordance with the laws of honor. On the other hand, he is never conscious of acting basely; if he were he would immediately reform since then his reason would show him the way to "curb his will." It is just that his passionate nature blinds his reason, which makes him to a certain extent incapable of differentiating between right and wrong. Almahide consistently reminds him of this flaw; she sums up his character in her last speech, calling him "rash . . . impotent of will," but she trusts his noble nature. His passion will burn out, and reason will take the upper hand: "You'll find the fire has but enlarged your space."

An interesting range of characters surrounds Almanzor and throws light on his own psychological portrait: Abdalla for instance is essentially noble, at least at the beginning; he has brought Almanzor to Boabdelin's aid and recognizes Almanzor's outstanding noble character. He also falls madly in love; goaded into betrayal by Lyndaraxa, he resists at first; he knows his reason should take the upper hand but finds himself incapable of resisting his passion. At least he is not basely ambitious, and if he turns traitor, it is only to win Lyndaraxa. The difference between him and Almanzor is that Abdalla is conscious of his betrayal of the dicta of honor, whereas Almanzor is never aware of not strictly obeying its requirements. Almanzor is given the benefit of the doubt that should he become aware of his shortcomings, he would immediately act accordingly. The real question of the play is, Will he or won't he? But Abdalla is irremediably lost, since knowing what he should do, he does not do it. His reason is not strong enough to overcome his passions.

Abdelmelech, likewise in love with Lyndaraxa, is also essentially noble. He tries to remind Abdalla of his duty to his king. But he also loves Lyndaraxa, and loves her too much for his own good; over and over he becomes the toy of Lyndaraxa, who makes of him what she wants. In a way he is a greater slave to his passions than Abdalla, since Lyndaraxa, promised to him, betrays him in favor of Abdalla and since he is at all times conscious of Lyndaraxa's ambitious and low nature. Abdalla loves her too much to see any fault in her, but Abdelmelech knowing her nature, still cannot help loving her. He is therefore the weaker of the two.

Boabdelin is weak, inglorious in battle, incapable of generosity, and a slave of his passion for Almahide, for although she does not love him, he will still have her.

Zulema, treacherous and with no ethical sense whatsoever, is capable of only the lowest passions: envy, treachery, betrayal, and lust in lieu of love. It is he who would relegate reason to old age, youth having nothing to do with it.

The pattern of absolute honor is Ozmyn. He has killed Benzayda's brother, but only in self-defense; he is extremely valorous in battle and is the only one capable of standing comparison to Almanzor in that respect. His love for Benzayda is extremely pure and is repaid in kind. Torn between the duty to obey his father and the duty he owes Benzayda, he finally chooses to follow his obligation to her. We can be sure it is not for selfish reasons but because this duty is the strongest: apart from the claim she has on him through her love, she has saved his life; and above all, she needs protection since her own father has rejected her and she has no one to turn to. Benzayda is as noble as Ozmyn and unselfishly urges him to abandon her and reconcile himself to his father.

The absolutely virtuous character is Almahide: too noble to feel real love for anyone but the fiery Almanzor, she is nevertheless in complete control of her passion. She knows her duty to her word, her father, and even Almanzor since she is the one who shows him the path of virtue.

In the second part of *The Conquest of Granada* there is no interesting new factor in characterization except for Almanzor. In the first part, he was noble, dedicated to honor but too easily swayed by passion. The question of whether he will ultimately attain his better self is left unanswered. The second part finds him oscillating like a pendulum between his better and his worse nature. The stronger he is at one moment, the weaker he is at another. He reaches his lowest point when Almahide is forced to attempt suicide in order to escape his repeated demands that she yield to him. Yet this vile behavior follows a seduction scene in which he stood adamant to all of Lyndaraxa's allurements. Eventually, guided by Almahide, he dominates his passions and acts unselfishly.

Aureng-Zebe, the hero of Dryden's so-called last heroic play is a near perfect pattern of virtue. Not once during the whole play does he act basely. He is at all times what we were told of him at the beginning of the play: "By no strong passion swayed, except his love." No matter how strong his love for Indamora, filial duty comes first, and he will do nothing to take Indamora away from his father. Without question he feels passion—love, anger, jealousy— but he is not "swayed" by passion. Though fate and his father relentlessly keep pushing him around, his only reaction is a sort of

despair, a bitter skepticism. Yet this skepticism is never strong
enough to make him perform even one act which would not conform to the strict requirements of honor: he is a skeptic but not
a cynic. And even his skepticism is only temporary; at the end of
the play he is reconciled with his former ideals. His jealousy of
Indamora cannot be considered a noble virtue. It is the only blemish
of his character, but it does not lead to wrongdoing. It does not
prompt him to betrayal or murder or any act unworthy of a hero;
it results only in what he himself calls a "quarrel." He really considers this jealousy a proof of the intensity of his passion.

There is no character in the play worthier than Aureng-Zebe.
Even Indamora is not so worthy; she has a few blemishes of her
own. She lures Morat on for Aureng-Zebe's sake; she takes advantage of Arimant's love for her; and she is afraid to die, even though
she thinks Aureng-Zebe is dead. Apart from that she is perfect—
true to her honor and to her love.

The Emperor, essentially noble, is ruled by his passion for Indamora. Though his reason is there to tell him what is right or
wrong, his passion is too strong to be overruled by his reason. He is
his noble self once more at the end when, ruled by his better nature,
he brings back Indamora to Aureng-Zebe in spite of the fact that he
still loves her.

The characterization of Morat follows the same pattern as that
of the Emperor: ruled by his baser passions, he eventually sees the
light and dies redeemed.

CHAPTER 3

THE ARCHETYPE

IT IS CLEAR, from what has preceded, that the different heroes of the heroic plays have much in common; they belong to a type which can be recognized very easily and should not be hard to delineate. Before doing so, however, there is a distinction which, though essential, does not seem to have been established by the majority of the critics who have dealt with the question—the distinction between the heroic hero as a type ideally conceived and the actual hero of a heroic play. Very often a critic will discuss indifferently some qualities of the heroic hero taken in general, ideally, or applied to the particular hero of one of the plays. In many instances the distinction is irrelevant, but not always.

For instance, *The Conquest of Granada* is one of Dryden's better-known plays; the hero is Almanzor; Almanzor is heroic. What happens is that a great number of critics, speaking of the heroic hero in general, will look for distinctive features in Almanzor and, focusing on the hero of a single well-known play, make of him the prototype of the genre. The method may be fruitful in some instances but not in others. In Almanzor's case, his ranting, for instance, is made by such critics a necessary feature of the heroic hero; but only two other major characters belong to the ranting type: Montezuma in *The Indian Queen* (but not in *The Indian Emperor*), and Maximin in *Tyrannic Love*. Maximin is not a hero, and his ranting is actually an exteriorization of his villainy; that leaves only Montezuma. When two heroes out of five rant, it is clear that ranting cannot be made a necessary feature of the heroic hero. It is only when a quality is found in all the heroes of the plays—and only in them—that we can say that it characterizes them. For instance, all the heroes are brave in battle, but so are

Morat, Maximin, Odmar, and Abdalla, who are by no means "heroic" heroes. The hero is never afraid of death, but neither are many of the villains: Maximin, the villain par excellence, is certainly not a coward. Consequently, courage and disdain of death are not specific characteristics of the hero.

As the summaries in the preceding chapter make plain, there is one major common trait of character which distinguishes the heroic hero from the others: his dominion, or eventual dominion, over his passion or passions. This is the one feat that a villain is never capable of (Traxalla in *The Indian Queen*, Zulema, Maximin); or if he is, it is only after he has brought upon himself disaster and destruction by his subjection to passion (Zempoalla, Montezuma in *The Indian Emperor*, Abdalla, Almeria, Morat).

Honor, passion, reason, seem to be the poles of attraction of all the major characters, whether heroes or villains. A hero will control his passion and act according to honor; a villain will let his passion loose and forsake his honor. The conflict is not really between passion and honor, however, but between reason and passion. If a character's reason is strong enough to curb his passion, he will have no difficulty in following the demands of honor. If it is too weak, he is lost. Over and over this law is stressed by heroes and villains alike. Dominated by passion, a character is a villain; dominated by reason, he is a hero. Honor or dishonor is the necessary consequence of the presence or absence of reason: this is why it is very often difficult to distinguish between these two concepts. Honor being a necessary consequence of reason, the characters use the terms interchangeably.

This confusion, which many critics have taken over, is made apparent in Almanzor again (this character in many ways is responsible for having led a number of critics astray). Almanzor idolizes honor; his devotion to honor is acknowledged by friend and foe alike; but though he believes he is acting according to honor, he is in fact betraying it because he is led astray by his passionate nature (as Almahide tells him). Once his passion is overcome, his sense of values is re-established. In fact, the way a character becomes honorable is often childishly portrayed: by means of an argumentative dialogue, in which the better character logically argues with the weaker one and convinces him of his error. The weaker one, shown the way, becomes a better person. This is true of heroes: Almanzor is convinced by Almahide, Porphyrius by Berenice. It is also true of villains: Morat—a fratricide, an in-

grate, ambitious, and unfaithful—needs only one ratiocinative con-
versation with Indamora to be won over to honor.

This control over the passions is really the touch-stone by which
everything is judged and regulated: a passion is not in itself
wrong or right. Neither is its intensity an indication: Maximin does
not love St. Catherine more than Berenice loves Porphyrius, but
Berenice controls her passion whereas Maximin does not. Her
passion is admirable; his, beastly. Nor does the object of a passion
have anything to do with the quality of that passion. A perfect
character is often loved by villains: St. Catherine is loved by
Maximin, Montezuma by Zempoalla, Cortez by Almeria, Almahide
by Zulema. Abdalla's love for Lyndaraxa is beautiful, but his
subjection to it is not. Almahide is loved by Almanzor, Zulema,
and Boabdelin; these last two feel only contemptible love. Almanzor's eventually becomes a beautiful one.

As a matter of fact, the quality of a given passion changes
according to whether it is controlled or not: Odmar's love for
Alibech was noble to start with and made him accomplish admirable
feats; as soon as he abandons himself to revenge and rage, his
love becomes nothing but lust. On the other hand, Almanzor's love
for Almahide, once he is capable of dominating his passions, loses
all physical character and becomes a noble inspiration.

Consequently we can only arrive at a conclusion directly opposite
to that held by most of the critics reviewed in the introduction.
We have to disagree with Chase when he affirms that "the distinctive feature of heroic love is that it nullifies all other ideals
in the lover, and makes him its absolute slave," and that "honor is
only speciously an important feature, as, notwithstanding the usual
connotations with it of certain ideals, the heroic play was too late
a growth to have the element of honor either of great extent or of
vital nature." [1] Chase stresses this point over and over again:

Heroic love is not a high and ennobling passion, but one which has the
great and distinctive peculiarity, that it sanctions a violation of all moral
laws wherever they are opposed to its free sweep and range, although,
when not conflicting with love, they are recognized as laws to which
man owes allegiance, and ideals of conduct toward which we should
work.[2]

J. W. Tupper is essentially of the same opinion. He holds that what
characterizes the heroes of the heroic plays is "their contempt for
the impossible and their overwhelming desire to attain their ends.

They scorn opposition, are utterly without fear, and in their most frenzied moods fly in the face of the powers above . . . the hero of the heroic play is first and always a lover, and his heroism is directed invariably towards the attainment of his love." [3] If we review the list of heroes, we shall find that few fit the description: Guyomar, Cortez, Porphyrius, Aureng-Zebe contradict it; even Almanzor spends most of his time protecting Boabdelin and restoring Almahide to her lawful possessor.

One of the consequences of holding love as supreme is to foster the error of opposing love and honor; many critics seem to imply that there is a conflict between them and that the hero is supposed to follow one or the other, to make a choice. This error is strengthened by the fact that love is more often than not the only passion that seems to animate all characters—heroes and villains alike. A confusion, like the one between honor and reason, quite understandably follows: the pervading passion being love, the ideal being honor—love and honor are opposed instead of passion and reason.

But as even a casual reading of any of the plays shows, the hero is never subjected to such a choice: Montezuma in *The Indian Queen* does not have to choose between Orazia and honor; as a matter of fact, dominated by anger and pride, he nearly loses his love; for him love and honor are on the same side of the fence. The problem seems rather for him to become worthy of his love by dominating his baser instincts and consequently acting according to the laws of honor. Almanzor does not have to choose between his love and his honor. At no moment is the problem raised in these terms; on the contrary, in order to be worthy of his love, he is called upon over and over again to master the various passions to which he is subject: anger, pride, jealousy, and lust. As for Aureng-Zebe, he has nothing to conquer except a few bouts with jealousy. Very passionate, but always in control of his passions, he is both a great lover and very honorable. As a matter of fact, love seems to be the necessary consequence of honor, as honor is the necessary consequence of reason, since the hero, once he has attained perfection, is always rewarded by the love of the perfect heroine.

Tupper, for instance, argues for the opposition of love and honor: "It is not till we reach the heroic play that we find a recognized opposition of love to honor, and then love is given the preference." [4] So also argues Margaret Sherwood: "Of these two sentiments, love

and honour, love is the more important. . . . In case of conflict between love and honour, love always triumphs." [5] It is true that each heroic play ends with love triumphant; but it also ends with honor triumphant; as a matter of fact, love triumphs because honor triumphs. The error results from equating love and passion, and using both terms interchangeably, as with honor and reason; whereas passion versus reason is correct, love versus honor is not. This is why critics eventually contradict themselves in the conclusions they draw: for instance, Tupper, in spite of the fact that he believes in a conflict between love and honor, has to admit that "in few of these plays does the conflict ever resolve itself in an absolute choice between love and honour." [6] Mildred Hartsock takes the opposition of love and reason for granted, though she points out that "in Dryden's plays, the dualism between passion and reason is, with few exceptions, purely nominal." However, she arrives at this conclusion by holding the view that passion is supreme over reason: "The characters in Dryden's plays are in the grip of devastating emotions, the laws of which are categorical, the force of which is irresistible." It is relevant that all of Miss Hartsock's illustrations are drawn from villains, though she seems to speak for both heroes and villains: "But although they [the heroes] and others overcome every physical obstacle and enjoy freedom from external restraints . . . they inevitably fall victims to their own passion." [7] This statement is very misleading. If she means that the hero can feel strong passion, she is right; but the word "victim" is inappropriate: the hero (unlike the villain) is never the victim of his passion, but its conqueror; he first overcomes it for honor's sake and then is rewarded by its fulfillment. This is why the only passion that animates heroes is love; love indeed can be a devastating passion; but controlled by reason it becomes pure and noble (very often Platonic)— the noble passion par excellence.

If this interpretation of the hero has any validity, it also contradicts that portion of Dryden criticism which considers both heroic tragedy and the hero as essentially romantic manifestations. Bonamy Dobrée is the principal exponent of this trend in the criticism of the heroic tragedy:

The dramatists of the day were trying to express romantic ideas in a form specially evolved for the classical. . . . What is curious about Restoration Tragedy is, that however much it may conform to classical order, the passions expressed in it are nearly always romantic passions:

in it, the limitations of human nature, one might say of nature, are disregarded and even flaunted.[8]

In his latest study of Dryden, Dobrée is still of the same opinion: "Emotions, states of mind, which are to the final degree romantic, are tailored into, or at least partly wear, severe classical garb. . . . Be prepared to enter a world of absolute emotions." [9]

Granted that the word "romantic" is complex, misleading, and subject to numerous interpretations, yet it has a fairly definite and accepted connotation when opposed to "classic." Having reached the conclusion that the hero (who as everybody agrees dominates the heroic play) is essentially characterized by submission to the dictates of reason, we can only call the term "romantic" as applied to the heroic play a misnomer. Dobrée himself defines what he means by "romantic" when he discusses Dryden's poetry: "There is then, in his poetry, none of the yearning of the Romantics, the reachings out after the impalpable in the attempt to grasp the inapprehensible: this vivid, actual imagination plays around the actions and passions of men and women as they live out their lives, in soul as well as in body." [10] This is apparently what Dobrée finds in Dryden: romanticism in the heroic plays, antiromanticism in the rest of his poetry. He does not seem to have been puzzled by the question of how an author can be completely romantic in one part of his work and antiromantic in another.

My conclusion is that such a contradiction, were it possible in any author, does not at any rate exist in Dryden. If we take up Dobrée's image, we can only reverse it and call the emotions, ideas, and states of mind "classical" and the garb "romantic." The hero, rather than being a wolf in sheep's clothing, is a sheep in wolf's clothing. This is the impression we get when we take a close look at the nature of the "reason" which stands supreme among the hero's ideals. The plot summaries show that this reason is not the overpowering, absolute, and infallible faculty which leads to all knowledge and reveals what is right and wrong. It is not the goddess of the French Revolution, and man is not a god because he possesses reason. Rather, this reason is a limited faculty which helps direct man's steps in everyday life; it is Hobbes's and Locke's reason; in other words, it is common sense. In Dryden's heroic plays, far from being the absolute faculty, it is only an instrument which, properly used, helps the hero conform to honor.

If we now examine the notion of honor, there, too, we find very little that can be qualified as romantic. The nature of the concept of honor in Dryden's time is a very interesting question, but apart from the fact that it has been ably treated elsewhere, it is a question that is outside the scope of this study.[11] What is relevant is the nature of honor in Dryden's plays in relation to the hero, and there we find that honor consists essentially of a set of rules or different sets of rules. Love, friendship, duty to king and country— all are minutely regulated, and there is no problem as to the obligations they create for the hero; each has a code which the hero is supposed to follow faithfully. Not only is he supposed to follow the code, but the implication seems to be that he is a hero in direct proportion to his adherence to that code; the better he obeys the rules, the more "heroic" he is. When a "heroic" hero in Dryden's plays does the right thing, it is never because of an inner prompting, the fulfillment of the inner self, but rather because it is what is held to be right by the social structure which surrounds him.

In the "heroic" hero we find the submission of the individual to the dictates of the tribe. Not once does the hero ever really question any of the duties imposed on him. This complete devotion, submission, even blindness—this total commitment of the self is what has made some critics speak of passion. But there is no need to stretch the point and show how unromantic this sort of passion is. The "heroic" hero has no need for motives; he knows what he must do; his only problem is to do it. We may characterize him best by calling him the anti-Hamlet hero. Hamlet's "honor" requires him to kill Claudius; no other "duty" or "love" or external obstacle really stops him from avenging his father. Yet it takes him five acts to do it, and then only as the result of a spontaneous gesture caused by his mother's murder. The searching, the questioning, the indecision are certainly not the "heroic" hero's forte. Aureng-Zebe, the closest to Hamlet among the heroes, awaiting death, gives in four lines the gist of the "to be or not to be" soliloquy:

> Distrust, and darkness of a future state,
> Make poor mankind so fearful of their fate.
> Death, in itself, is nothing; but we fear,
> To be we know not what, we know not where.
>
> (IV,i)

But this speech is not functional like its original; it does not portray a state of mind which directly or indirectly influences the actions of the character who utters it; it is only a pretty but gratuitous ornament.

This lack of need for inner motivation is what makes the "heroic" hero essentially a man of action. Whether he is doing what he is supposed to do, or momentarily succumbing to his passions, the hero is in a perpetual state of action. He is never busy looking into himself, analyzing his motives, his states of mind, his passions. This has been done for him by others, by the social structure that surrounds him, and he has accepted its demands once and for all. For this reason we should not be surprised to find that the "heroic" play consists of a series of superimposed incidents following closely one upon another; given the hero, it could be nothing else. Hence, we cannot agree with those critics who find no relation between plot and character in the heroic play. Speaking of the construction of the heroic plays, J. W. Tupper says: "It is not truly dramatic like that of Shakespeare's tragedies, where the action is in part developed from character; but it is skillfully suited to theatrical effectiveness." [12] Margaret Sherwood also believes that "strictly speaking they [the heroic plays] contain no ruling idea working its way through character into action." [13] Our conclusion on the contrary, is that this type of plot is the direct consequence of the hero's character.

The absence of inner conflict, duly and repeatedly noted by critics, is another consequence of this special way in which the hero's character is conceived. A man whose paramount virtue is or should be complete submission to various codes of honor has no business with internal conflict. The hero is never face to face with one major inner problem. His task is rather to stand up to and overcome a succession of mainly physical obstacles which at most symbolize the continuous achievement of the hero: his domination over self, the constant exercise of will, which is only directed toward the fulfillment of the dicta of the tribe.

This submission to accepted norms is what makes it difficult to accept the repeated parallelism which the critics find between the "heroic" hero and Marlowe's Tamburlaine. J. W. Tupper likens Dryden's heroes to Marlowe's (Tamburlaine, Faust, Barabas); the main difference between the two types he finds only in the treatment of love: "They differ, however, in their relation to love. The Marlovian hero treats love as secondary to the attainment of power. . . . But the hero of the heroic play is first and always a lover." [14]

Were it correct, this difference in itself would be extremely important, but we have already seen that the hero of the heroic plays is first concerned with honor and only afterwards with love. B. J. Pendlebury, on the one hand, holds that the hero of the heroic play is subject to "heroic" love, "most improperly so termed, since, though it inspires the hero's valour, it makes him an abject slave to his own passion, and to the caprice of his mistress." [15] But, on the other hand, he likens Dryden's heroes to Marlowe's and states that "the dream of power beyond the bounds of common experience seems to have attracted Dryden and his audience as much as it attracted Marlowe and the Elizabethans." [16]

Almanzor again is probably responsible for this misconception; he does wear a few feathers borrowed from Tamburlaine, but the two characters are actually poles apart. Essentially, they have nothing in common except physical valor. Tamburlaine's drive for power, the "aspiring mind," the climb after "knowledge infinite" are certainly not Almanzor's. Tamburlaine takes his destiny in his own hands and shapes it; his defiance of the gods or God is no mere rhetorical flight; he is bent on reaching the ultimate possibilities of man (symbolized in the "earthly crown" as opposed to the heavenly), the border where man and God merge, and as the "scourge of God" he substitutes himself for divine power. Tamburlaine obeys no law but Tamburlaine's. What a far cry from Almanzor who, misled by his tempestuous nature, finally becomes the paragon of submission—submission to the laws of honor, of love, of country, of one's better self—and who ends ten acts of dilly-dallying by shouting, "Live and Reign, / Great Ferdinand and Isabel of Spain." Tamburlaine's "mind" could not have conceived such a pitiful goal; Almanzor's "reason" can think of nothing better.

In a recent unpublished dissertation M. W. Alssid, after opposing what he calls the "present body of criticism," examines Dryden's heroic plays and comes to the conclusion that they create a "world picture":

Fundamentally, this picture expresses the persistent conflict between characters who embody heroic virtue . . . and characters who embody satanic vice. Against "Hell's Dire Agents," the hero struggles and in his ultimate victory over demonic forces, this man, who is "more than man," resolves in himself and for his generation the permanent and universal symbols of a quasi-human, quasi-divine perfection.[17]

Whatever the arguments which Alssid uses (on the whole rather far-fetched), they are essentially in contradiction to the picture which emerges from the plot summaries. The characters are not divided into good and bad, and what is more important, the contest is not between a good and a bad character. In *The Indian Emperor* Guyomar has nothing to do with Almeria, and Cortez actually ends up being grateful to her. In *The Conquest of Granada,* if we decide that Lyndaraxa is the bad character personifying vice, Almanzor meets her in one scene and does not need to fight her off since not for one moment is he under her charm; nor is there any contest between Almanzor and Boabdelin either. In *Tyrannic Love* Porphyrius and Maximin are not opposed; St. Catherine is opposed to Maximin; but can one speak of contest, of "ultimate victory"? St. Catherine will have nothing to do with Maximin and does not even try to convert him; on the contrary, she needs him in order to become a martyr and a saint. As for Maximin, all he feels for her is lust, and he lives and dies a man subject to his passions. If St. Catherine had changed him in some way, then there might have been "victory"; as it is, if St. Catherine personifies good and Maximin vice, no victory of virtue over vice is personified. As a matter of fact, Dryden's own analysis of Maximin is quite explicit: "The part of Maximin . . . was designed by me to set off the character of St. Catherine." [18] It shows that Dryden is not interested in a contest between the two, but in portraying virtue and vice as such.

Actually, there is no contest or conflict properly speaking, but rather a constant exercise of the will, of dominion over oneself on the part of the hero; the only conflict is a conflict between passion and reason, and that conflict takes place in the hero's own self. As a matter of fact, when we speak of the hero, the word "conflict" is too strong; passion and reason do not tear at each other in the hero's soul; passion is given free reign as long as it is curbed by reason. The struggle resolves itself into a continuous exercise of reason.

What gives the picture of "vice versus virtue" even less validity is the fact that characters are not divided into good and bad. On the contrary, if we look at any play, we find a close gradation in the range of characters, starting with the perfect and leading to the villain. As we have seen, the perfect "heroic" character is not always the hero: in *The Indian Queen*, the perfect "heroic" character is Acacis; in *The Indian Emperor*, it is Guyomar; in *The Conquest of Granada*, it is Ozmyn. As a rule, the heroine is virtue incarnate, and she certainly undergoes no contest with vice (Almahide, Berenice, Orazia). Following close on the heels of the perfect character, we have the near perfect one, usually the hero (Montezuma in *The Indian Queen,* Almanzor, Porphyrius in *Tyrannic Love*). This character knows where his duty lies, is momentarily misled by passion, but with the help of the virtuous character (generally the heroine) he overcomes his passion and attains perfection. Next comes the essentially noble character who, however, is the slave of an overruling passion which he cannot control though he knows he should; this character is generally the old king (Montezuma in *The Indian Emperor,* the Emperor in *Aureng-Zebe*) in love with a much younger woman; in *The Conquest of Granada* it is Abdalla or Abdelmelech; in *Tyrannic Love* it is Valeria who loves Porphyrius too much for her own good. Further down the hierarchy we find the character given over to passion who could still be retrievable; in some cases he is retrieved (Morat in *Aureng-Zebe*); in others he is lost (Odmar in *The Indian Emperor*). Whatever the outcome, this character is doomed to die, either justly punished (Odmar) or because he has seen the light too late and should be punished for his previous crimes (Morat). Finally, we reach the villain, a slave to his passion or passions, and we regularly witness his downfall; nevertheless, sometimes even this villain is won over to virtue at the end (Zempoalla, Almeria).

What this gradation in characterization shows is that each and every character undergoes for himself his own private battle between passion and reason; and he is either victorious or vanquished in direct relation to the amount of reason he is capable of. Using a very gross simplification, we could say that Dryden for his characterization starts from one essential character, then adds the two components, reason and passion. The villains he overloads with passion; then working his way up, he adds less passion and more reason until he reaches the perfect character: reason in complete mastery of passion. This is why some critics have been able to say that there is not much difference between villains and heroes in Dryden's plays.[19] At any given moment, a hero is liable to become a villain if he abandons himself to passion; and a villain can at any time become virtuous if he curbs his passion.

It is therefore misleading to say (like Thomas H. Fujimura and others) that the theme of the heroic plays is the struggle between love and honor: "It can be shown that even the central theme, the struggle between love and honor, is strongly naturalistic in conception." [20] The struggle is not between love and honor, but between passion and reason. Fujimura is aware of the possible confusion in terminology, but he seems to apply it only to reason and honor; he contends that honor "replaces reason as the guide to virtue, and . . . is nothing more or less than one of the dominant passions." [21] It is true that the commitment to honor is passionate, but at no moment is the relationship between reason and honor disregarded, except precisely where the hero, misled by his passions, thinks he is acting according to honor, but in fact is not (Almanzor helping Abdalla, for instance).

Later on in his study, Fujimura defines what he means by honor: "And honor, identified with pride, anger, self-aggrandizement, and glory, is a naturalistic notion." [22] In no way do the plays support this statement; a hero can be rightly proud of his better self, but at no moment is the sin of excessive pride accepted as such. Montezuma in *The Indian Queen* brings all kinds of misfortune upon himself and those he loves because of excessive pride. Pride is Almanzor's major shortcoming; it is the only fault Almahide sees in him and gently chides him for:

> Might I not make it as my last request,
> That you would somewhat of your fierceness hide,
> That inborn fire—I do not call it pride?
> (IV,i)

Pride may be a common attribute of heroic heroes, but it is only when they subdue it that they act according to the laws of honor. As to "anger," it fares no better than pride. Rarely is it Aristotle's "ireful virtue"; more often than not it is a defect the hero must overcome: "Compose these wilde Distempers in your breast;/ Anger, like madness, is appeas'd by rest," says Acacis to Montezuma (I, i). Almanzor's predisposition to anger is certainly one of his major shortcomings; indignant at Boabdelin's treatment of Almahide, he refuses to help him:

> ALMAHIDE: Unkind Almanzor, how am I betrayed
>   Betrayed by him in whom I trusted most!
> ALMANZOR: Oh, I have erred; but fury made me blind.
> (III,i)

As to "self-aggrandizement," if we agree that passion is to be subdued, then no case can be made for it. "Glory" raises a different problem; if we give it today's meaning, it could be a means to self-aggrandizement, but Jean Gagen, partly answering Fujimura's article, retraces the history of the concept of honor and shows the "intimate connection between self-esteem and public esteem." Because of this connection, "a gentleman was obliged to protect his reputation, good name, credit, or fame, even at the cost of his life. . . . It was right and proper to expect to have his merits recognized." [23] Glory is a natural consequence of virtue since "the virtues which the man of honor was obliged to practice, were primarily public virtues." When glory is a means to private ends, it is usually called ambition. Lyndaraxa, for instance, is ambitious:

> Why would I be a queen? . . .
> Yes! I avow the ambition of my soul,
> To be that one to live without control.
>   (II,i)

We can only reach a conclusion directly opposed to Fujimura's view that "Dryden's heroic plays, then, extol the primacy of passion, and sex is glorified as the most powerful of human passions." [24] Dryden's heroic plays extol the primacy of reason, and though sex may be the most powerful of human passions, it certainly is not glorified in the plays.

We have no reason to doubt that this primacy of reason was essentially Dryden's underlying idea in all the heroic plays, and we have to disagree with Bonamy Dobrée when he writes:

Indeed, if we seek in Dryden some definite message, or some special attitude we shall seek in vain. If this is a defect in him, it is one which he shares with Shakespeare. All that we can feel for certain in considering the two, is a difference in the wholeness of their attitude; we know that though both of them approached life in a multitude of ways, they approached it at different levels. We may suggest the difference roughly by saying that Shakespeare was metaphysical where Dryden was moral.[25]

Even if we leave aside the question of comparing and, *a fortiori*, likening Dryden and Shakespeare, there still seems to be a contradiction between what Dobrée says at the beginning of the quotation and the conclusion he arrives at—that there is no "definite message" or "special attitude" in Dryden and that Dryden is "moral." Anything "moral" implies the existence of a standard of values. It means condemnation or approval, the adoption of an "attitude" in accordance with that standard of values which by its very existence demands a "message." What Dryden's "attitude" and "message"

are in the heroic plays has already been described at length. As
a matter of fact, one could justly reproach Dryden for the very
repetitiousness of that message, the lack of diversity in his "controlling idea." It is this consistency of what Dryden calls the "fable"
that is partly responsible for the monotony of which critics (and
most probably readers) complain in Dryden's plays. "The relation
of plot to character is casual, not inevitable; the hero of one play
differs very little from one of another," says J. W. Tupper."[26] If
there is no relation between plot and character, why should there
be no diversity in characterization? If Tupper's second statement
does not contradict his first, it still does not explain it. But if
characterization and plot are closely linked, then given a certain
plot, or "fable," the hero can only belong to one type in all the
plays. We have Dryden's own word that this is the method he
followed:

> For the moral (as Bossu observes) is the first business of the poet, as
> being the groundwork of his instruction. This being formed, he con-
> trives such a design, or fable, as may be most suitable to the moral;
> after this he begins to think of the persons whom he is to employ in
> carrying on his design; and gives them the manners which are most
> proper to their several characters. The thoughts and words are the last
> parts, which give beauty and colouring to the piece."[27]

That plot and moral are closely linked in Dryden's mind is irre-
futable. In the quotation just cited, taken from his essay, "A Parallel
Between Poetry and Painting" (1695), he calls the moral the
groundwork of a poem. In the preface to *Troilus and Cressida*
(1679), he held the same opinion: ". . . 'tis the moral that directs
the whole action of the play to one centre; and that action or
fable is the example built upon the moral, which confirms the truth
of it to our experience: when the fable is designed, then, and not
before, the persons are to be introduced, with their manners,
characters, and passions."[28] For Dryden then, "moral" is the same as
"plot" or "fable," the plot being only the physical means by which
a moral is carried out; and character is part of the plot, an illustration of the moral. The moral being uniform, the character cannot
vary either. As Pendlebury says, "There are only slight variations
in the types and it would be almost impossible to distinguish the
speeches of one hero from those of another, or indeed from those
of a villain."[29] But like many other critics, Pendlebury attributes this
to a lack of ability in characterization on Dryden's part: "Dryden

certainly had the ability to invent an interesting story, whereas his power of creating character was slight." [30] Our contention is that, whatever his ability, Dryden is limited or handicapped in his characterization precisely because of the one moral—and consequent plot—he had chosen.

We have tried not to rely too heavily on Dryden's own criticism as direct proof for what we find or are supposed to find in his plays. Dryden's critical works span the whole of his literary career; he wrote widely and diversely on every literary topic of interest to him. He was not consistent in what he wrote since he treated a given topic at different times and from different points of view. It would certainly be foolish to reproach him for that. When critics attempt to judge Dryden's work in the light of his criticism, they are more often than not dismayed by his lack of consistency: "If there is on the whole, growth toward clearer vision and broader views, there is to the end, a lack of finality in what he says," concludes Margaret Sherwood.[31] When in need of a cohesive body of criticism, some critics limit themselves to one time period, or to a limited number of works, a method which is at the very least arbitrary.[32] It is rather easy to have Dryden on one's side since at one time or another he actually has been. Consequently, we shall refer to Dryden's criticism only to the extent that his opinion reinforces conclusions already reached; he will be asked to complete a picture, not to be its main pattern.

In short, a study of the plot and characterization in Dryden's heroic plays leads to a clear picture of the psychology of the hero: a passionate man who is, or will be eventually, in complete mastery of his passion by means of his reason. That same reason is his safe conduct to honor, which consists of absolute submission to one or more sets of rules, worked out for the individual by the social structure surrounding him.

What gives validity to this final picture of the hero is that it fits perfectly, on the one hand, the period in which and for which it was created, and on the other, Dryden's own psychological evolution.

CHAPTER 4

DRYDEN'S PSYCHOLOGY
AND THE HISTORICAL MILIEU

ANY ATTEMPT TO give a fairly complete picture of the intellectual thought contemporary with Dryden would be an ambitious, indeed impossible, endeavor which will not be undertaken here. There are, however, two major components of seventeenth- and eighteenth-century thought which have been widely recognized and studied: the hegemony of reason and the strong current of skepticism.

The "Age of Reason" is a familiar enough appellation, though the French would rather apply it to their own seventeenth century, and the English to the neoclassical movement of the eighteenth. That the nature of reason is not the same in both centuries has been widely recognized:

The eighteenth century takes reason in a different and more modest sense. It is no longer the sum total of "innate ideas" given prior to all experience, which reveal the absolute essence of things. Reason is now looked upon rather as an acquisition than as a heritage. It is not the treasury of the mind in which the truth like a minted coin lies stored; it is rather the original intellectual force which guides the discovery and determination of Truth.[1]

Something happened between the seventeenth and eighteenth centuries to accomplish that change. The following is, of course, a gross simplification of what took place, and this sort of analysis is always very hazardous; but sometimes the clarification gained justifies whatever distortion the final picture undergoes. What occurred was the superposition of skeptical thought on Cartesianism. That Cartesianism carried within itself its own demise is beside the point for our purpose. We are simply interested in identifying these

35

two currents and in showing that the effect of the one on the other really took place at the end of the seventeenth century, approximately at the time when Dryden was writing his tragedies. Our contention is that these tragedies reflect not only both trends of thought but also the influence of skepticism on reason. In a masterful and at the same time delightful work, Paul Hazard has isolated and studied this movement which he calls "La Crise de la Conscience Européenne." [2]

Hazard limits this period to the years 1680–1715, though he acknowledges the arbitrary nature of the dates, which are only convenient from the standpoint of literary works particularly representative of that *crise*. We have only to remember that Spinoza, Fontenelle, Locke, Leibnitz, Bossuet, Fénelon, and especially Bayle wrote during this period, to realize that a revolution in European thought was taking place. With reference to that period Hazard writes:

Entre la Renaissance dont elle procède directement et la Révolution française, qu'elle prépare, il n'y en a pas de plus importante dans l'histoire des idées. A une civilisation fondée sur l'idée du devoir, les devoirs envers Dieu, les devoirs envers le prince, les "nouveaux philosophes" ont essayé de substituer une civilisation fondée sur l'idée du droit; les droits de la Conscience individuelle, les droits de la critique, les droits de la raison, les droits de l'homme et du citoyen. [3]

This idea of duty by which Hazard characterizes European thought before the 1680's is precisely what we have encountered at every turn in Dryden's heroic tragedies; and the concept of right which he applies to eighteenth-century thought is what is completely absent from these plays. The hero is the one who does his duty, by his king or his country, friend or love, father or son, but certainly not by his own self. What we have found is the denial of the self rather than its realization. Whenever the hero gets something for himself (the love of the heroine as a rule), it is as a reward for submitting every natural or instinctive impulse to the pressure of reason, but never as a right that is won against contrary odds.

This characteristic would tend to make Dryden's plays essentially seventeenth-century manifestations. But it is precisely in the nature of that reason which governs everything that we find reflected the undermining influence of the skepticism of the period: for that reason is no longer the Cartesian reason, though it still carries one of its main attributes—universality. As found in the plays we examined, reason is still Cartesian in that it seems to be a faculty that exists in any and all persons; in case of conflict, the only solution is to dominate one's passion, and thereby open the way to reason. Villain and hero refer to it in identical terms, and it is interchangeable from one person to another; when momentarily deprived of it, a hero acts like a villain, and when a villain is won over to reason, he attains "heroic" proportions. This reason is infallible; one has only to listen to it.

"To listen to it"—this is precisely the critical point at which reason in Dryden's plays is no more the Cartesian reason. Granted that Cartesian reason is universal, it is also personal—that is, used by the individual to work out his own issues and even the world's. It is the *cogito ergo sum* aspect of Cartesianism that is completely lacking in our "heroic" hero. Never does he use his own reasoning faculty to work out his own problems. Tamburlaine and especially his alter ego Faust, were closer to Cartesianism than Dryden's heroes. In Dryden, the "I think, therefore I am" is replaced by "I am because I do what I must." Essentially here, we have a distrust of personal reason rather than an exaltation of it; whatever exaltation there is, is reserved to other people's reason, or rather to society's rules and dicta which have withstood the test of time and need not be looked into and questioned. We are in the presence of a shifting of responsibility from the individual to society.[4] Reason is still there, but it is more a matter of exercise of the will than of common sense. The fact that the Cartesian virtue par excellence is also the exercise of the will does not contradict what has preceded. The problem is only a matter of emphasis. The Cartesian is the one who exercises his will in the light of his own reason, which is universal in that it is a common human attribute. Dryden's hero exercises his will in the light of rules and dicta issued for him by society which, if not infallible, is still more trustworthy than oneself. This slight distortion which the concept of reason undergoes in the heroic plays is what illustrates their skeptical aspect.

Neoclassical reason or common sense is usually linked with optimism. Francis Galloway speaks of "the optimism of the period" and insists on its corollary, the overall domination of common sense, though he points out some exceptions, among them Dryden:

There were always rebels against reason, for, as Swift knew, sanity and moderation have always had less general appeal than sentimentality and humbug. In the Prologue to *Tyrannick Love* (1669) Dryden proclaimed the right of men to be well deceived by heroic tragedy. Before he was in his grave the old gospel of Longinus, as interpreted by his disciple, Boileau, revealed the function of poetry to be the creation of ecstasy.[5]

One should obviously refer to what Dryden did, rather than what he said, to judge his work. As we have seen, "sanity" and "moderation" are the virtues most exalted in the heroic plays, both in word and action. Even if we refer to what Dryden has to say on his own *Tyrannic Love* (neither in the preface nor the prologue does he use the word "deceive"), we shall find that his aim is not to "deceive" the reader in the modern sense, but to lure him to whatever moral he wants to impose upon him:

I consider that pleasure was not the only end of poesie. . . . By the Harmony of words, we elevate the mind to a sense of Devotion, as our solemn Musick, which is inarticulate poesie, does in churches; and by the lively images of piety, adorned by action, through the senses, allure the soul: which while it is charmed in a silent joy of what it sees and hears, is struck at the same time with a secret veneration of things Celestial, and is wound up insensibly into the practice of that which it admires.[6]

In the light of the above, when Dryden "deceives" his readers, it is for the purpose of winning them over to reason; as Samuel Monk shows in his valuable study, *The Sublime in Eighteenth Century England,* the neoclassicists never considered the "creation of ecstasy" as the function of poetry.[7]

Boileau understood the sublime as a great thought capable of awakening strong emotions in the reader or the audience. The concept of the function of the drama as awakening emotions in the audience is at least as old as Aristotle. But these emotions in neoclassical criticism are not an end in themselves, only a means to an end. Longinus's key word is not ecstasy; it is "transport," the end being "high thoughts":

When, therefore, a thing is heard repeatedly by a man of intelligence, who is well versed in literature, and its effect is not to dispose the soul to high thoughts, and it does not leave in the mind more food for reflection than the words seem to convey, but falls, if examined carefully through and through, into disesteem, it cannot rank as true sublimity because it does not survive a first hearing. For that is really great which bears a repeated examination. . . .

Passion is not automatically part of the sublime; Longinus argues for it, but he does not put it first: "First and most important is the power of forming great conceptions. . . . Secondly, there is vehement and inspired passion." In short, "sublimity is the echo of a great soul." The end to be attained is "admiration":

In general, consider those examples of sublimity to be fine and genuine which please all and always. For when men of different pursuits, lives, ambitions, ages, languages, hold identical views on one and the same object, then that verdict which results, so to speak, from a concert of discordant elements makes our faith in the object of admiration strong and unassailable. . . . For it is not possible that men with mean and servile ideas and aims . . . should produce anything that is admirable and worthy of immortality. . . . Hence also a bare idea, by itself and without a spoken word, sometimes excites admiration just because of the greatness of soul implied.[8]

Undoubtedly, then, admiration and not ecstasy is the response that should be incited by sublimity. This is how the neoclassicists understood Longinus. "Ecstasy" was a later acquisition of the eighteenth century.

The heroic paraphernalia (rhetorical flights, rant, bustling action, accumulation of climaxes) is what Dryden uses to "transport" his audiences and win them over to an ideal of reason and submission. In the light of what we know of Dryden, it is impossible to make of him—as Galloway does—a rebel against reason. Though, as we have seen, his brand of reason is not typical of the early seventeenth century and even less the powerful tool which the eighteenth century made of it (Locke, Newton), it is still reason, but stripped of its optimistic connotation.

La doctrine cartésienne procurait une certitude, une securité; elle opposait au scepticisme une retentissante affirmation; elle démontrait l'existence de Dieu, l'immatérialité de l'âme; elle distinguait la pensée d'avec l'étendue, la noble idée d'avec la sensation; elle marquait la victoire de la liberté sur l'instinct; bref elle était un rempart contre le libertinage. Or voici qu'elle affermissait le libertinage et le renforçait. Car elle préconisait l'examen, la critique; elle exigeait impérieusement l'évidence, même en des matières jadis soustraites par l'autorité aux lois de l'évidence.[9]

It is this questioning which Cartesianism carries within itself that was eventually to be used against it. In most cases this questioning did not lead to either despair or Pyrrhonism; Spinoza, Leibnitz, the Cambridge Platonists, and especially Locke are instances of opposition to Pyrrhonism. Bayle, however, came very close to Pyrrhonism, and Pascal, the Cartesian thinker par excellence, could only escape despair through faith.

Dryden too had passed the point of questioning. A question implies an answer. In Dryden's plays the hero asks no questions, for he expects no answers. To question, to doubt, is too hazardous; one may come up with the wrong answers. When authority is present to guarantee security through the maintenance of a status quo, why risk worse evils? To support this status quo is, in fact, the "heroic" hero's vocation.

Once more let us refer to Dryden: "And I meddle not with others, being, for my opinion, of Montaigne's principles, that an honest man ought to be contented with that form of government, and with those fundamental constitutions of it, which he received from his ancestors and under which himself was born." [10] This attitude is, of course, characteristic of Pyrrhonism. Dryden's adherence to the status quo in political matters leads us to examine another aspect of the close relationship between the heroic tragedy and the period: the political and historical "moment."

We must go back approximately fifty years in time and cross the Channel to France. Then and there we witness the flowering of the French heroic tragedy. Corneille's *Le Cid*, a full-fledged representative of the genre, was first produced in 1636. What were the political circumstances before and at the time of *Le Cid*? In France, the second half of the sixteenth century was a period of great instability; religious wars, especially, brought France to the brink of total ruin. Weak kings and strong feudal lords kept the political scene in a state of constant effervescence. When Henri IV decided that "Paris vaut bien une messe" and turned Catholic to gain a crown, France under his reign began to breathe more freely. Slowly, patiently, Henri IV was working at rebuilding France in a climate of tolerance and was trying to provide every peasant with a fat hen for his Sunday cooking pot when he was assassinated by Ravaillac in 1610.

Once more France was in the hands of a child-king, his scheming Italian mother, and her paramours. Once more the vassals began tearing at the kingdom. But Richelieu with an iron hand and Machiavellian statesmanship crushed the vassals one by one, and worked for a united France under an absolute monarch. Richelieu was by no means loved: his scheming mind, his driving thirst for power, his greed (at his death he was supposedly the richest man in France not excepting the King) brought him nothing but hate, and the King, who obeyed him most readily, hated him most heartily.

But he was appreciated, and at his death in 1642, one year before the death of Louis XIII, his absence was keenly felt. Those who appreciated and accepted Richelieu were the very ones who went to the theatre and thrilled at Corneille's plays, for these plays were fulfilling their needs in the same manner as was Richelieu. Weary of quarrels, turmoil, uncertainty, and insecurity, they found in the heroic play an ideal of order, of duty, of submission to authority. They did not find any questioning or search for psychological motivations, and they did not care to find them. Furthermore, this ideal of duty to king, country, and God was couched in the most stirring rhetoric, illustrated by glorious feats of valor amid the bustle of war, which was part of the audience's everyday life; a nobleman was first of all a soldier, and counting the "noblesse de province," half of France belonged to the nobility.

When Richelieu died, his work was certainly not finished, and the Regency was far from feeling itself absolute. The Fronde, the impudent rabble of Paris, and especially that dashing and "heroic" cousin of his, the Prince de Condé, caused Louis XIV to go into hiding three times before a succession of able ministers consolidated his power and made of him "le Roi Soleil." During this entire period Corneille was the unquestioned master playwright, and the heroic tragedy thrived.

Let us now return to England. On the whole, the country had fared well during the second half of the sixteenth century under Elizabeth I. The seventeenth century, however, was far from maintaining whatever stability had been achieved in the late Tudor period. In fact, when England called back Charles II after the Commonwealth, the country was in much the same mood as that of France in 1610. The English had had their fill of wars, factions, and revolutions. They craved order, security, and authority. The heroic tragedy, in its own way, tried to provide exactly these elements: to present its audience with an ideal of order, of sanity, based on submission to social authority that exalted nothing more than the concept of duty. The glory, the excitement, the battles, the rhetorical flights were nothing but the "garb," which was meant only to stir the spectator and "lure" him over to duty.

In this near identity of political and historical circumstances surrounding the heroic tragedy both in France and in England lies probably the answer as to why Dryden wrote Cornelian plays in Racine's time. Corneille was still writing, of course, and writing the same kind of tragedies, but his popularity had declined. The decline was not based on the quality of his work; he was being faithful to his own genius and his own standards; his audience was not being faithful to him. It had gone over to Racine. Why? We believe that here the historical "moment" is very important. Monarchy was finally absolute. Order and security were everywhere. France had reached its apogee. Questions of authority, order, and submission were no longer paramount; they had been solved. The "noble" man was no more a fighting vassal, but a courtier tied to Versailles, with time on his hands—time enough to look into himself and into his passions, to indulge in minute psychological motivations, and to witness the devastation of souls rather than of kingdoms. Corneille was still writing for the audiences of the 1630's; he could not be appreciated by the French audiences of the 1670's. But he could be, in England, where the political atmosphere was the same as that of fifty years before in France, and where Dryden was producing his kind of drama.

Dryden knew Racine, but he never showed any sympathy or appreciation for his work. Dryden's attack on Racine in the Preface to *All for Love* is well known. "Thus their Hippolytus is so scrupulous in point of decency that he will rather expose himself to death than accuse his stepmother to his father." Dryden chooses (either purposely or not) to distort Hippolytus' motive: not to hurt his father. Moreover, Hippolytus did not know he would die, whereas Dryden in his own *Aureng-Zebe* makes the hero choose death rather than tell his father about Nourmahal's incestuous advances. The lack of appreciation of Racine by Dryden's contemporaries has been treated masterfully by Katherine Wheatley in *Racine and English Classicism*, in which she demonstrates that Racine has continued to be misunderstood by Anglo-Saxon critics and readers down to the present day: "It might be said that English neo-classicism completely passed over the Racinian moment in French classical tragedy." [11] Miss Wheatley believes it is because the "English read French theory in preference to French dramatists." Her nearly exhaustive research on French critical theory validates her point. Yet Corneille's dramatic work was read and appreciated, while Racine's was not. We believe that what we have called the historical "moment" played a decisive part in this question: English audiences misread Racine because they were not ready for him; they did not need him, whereas they still needed Corneille.

Our conclusion then is that Dryden was writing the kind of drama that not only pleased his audiences and embodied their needs, but also reflected some of the major problems which confronted the age.

If we turn now to Dryden himself, we shall find that the conclusions made earlier in this study do not conflict with his own psychological formation as we know it. The following is heavily indebted to Louis Bredvold's study of Dryden, which is now widely accepted by critics.[12] Essentially, Bredvold's well-known thesis is that Dryden was a skeptic whose Pyrrhonism drove him to conservatism in politics and to Catholicism through fideism in religion.

He [Dryden] lived in an age of philosophical skepticism; every reader of any pretensions to cultivation knew Montaigne and Charron intimately and almost every scholar has read Sextus Empiricus. Neither Dryden nor his age can be fully understood apart from this Pyrrhonism, diffused in every department of thought, lending itself to the most diverse purposes, appearing sometimes in strange guises.[13]

This statement, though essentially sound, is rather sweeping. Dryden's age was not solely an age of skepticism; Spinoza, Leibnitz, Locke, and even Hobbes were not skeptics. They certainly were not Pyrrhonists, yet Bredvold seems to use the two terms interchangeably. If they are to have the same meaning, then where does that leave libertinism? I believe that skepticism—an attitude that favored questioning and relied heavily on libertinism—was "diffused in every department of thought," but that Pyrrhonism— a philosophical system exhorting ultraconservatism—was not.

After tracing the traditions of skepticism in European thought down to Dryden's time, Bredvold studies the related philosophical systems of Hobbes's materialism, the Royal Society's philosophical attitudes, and Thomas Browne's skepticism in *Religio Medici*. He shows Dryden's affinity to the attitude of the Royal Society and concludes: "It was this distrust of reason, this philosophical skepticism that drove Dryden toward conservatism and authority in religion, and ultimately to the Catholic Church, just as his distrust of the populace was one reason for his increasing conservatism and Toryism in politics."[14] He next devotes a whole chapter to

Roman Catholic apologetics in England and stresses their heavy reliance on fideism even though fideism as such was considered a heresy by the church itself: "Roman Catholic propagandists, who were sensitive to the new intellectual atmosphere and desired to conduct their controversies with intellectual as well as social finesse, put their emphasis on fideism and traditionalism as never before." [15]

Bredvold gives Father Simon's *Histoire critique du Vieux Testament* a prominent place among the diverse influences affecting Dryden, as undoubtedly it did. Father Simon, whom Paul Hazard calls the "érudit" par excellence, the first great compiler, meant to deal a major blow to Protestantism by showing the unreliability of the Bible. That he was at the same time dealing an equally devastating blow to Roman Catholicism is a question that he seems to have overlooked. At any rate, Dryden understood both destructive aspects of the work, and his fideistic tendencies could only have been reinforced by it. Bredvold does not disregard the appeal that reason had for Dryden, but he contends that "the rationalistic tendency in Dryden evidently did not develop very freely or very far; it must inevitably have been inhibited by that Pyrrhonistic turn of his mind, indications of which are scattered throughout his writings." [16] He goes on to analyze in detail *Religio Laici* and *The Hind and the Panther*, showing how "both are basically skeptical and fideistic," and concludes that Dryden's "shifts of allegiance were all changes in the same direction, toward greater conservatism. . . . His assent to Catholicism was more in the nature of a retreat to an impregnable fortification when the more forward position had been proved untenable." [17]

Turning to Dryden's political position, Bredvold notes the close connection of conservatism and skepticism in politics. He shows how Dryden must have been attracted by Hobbes's absolutist political theory. But Dryden's very distrust of reason kept him from adhering to the theory of determinism underlying the concept of absolutism. He believed in authority and absolute monarchy, but we shall see later on how in the plays Dryden modifies this concept and purges it of all Hobbesianism. Noting the instances of Hobbesian absolutist theory, Bredvold says:

Dryden may be said to have reflected the political ideas of that philosopher Hobbes in his plays. . . . But it may be fairly questioned whether this strained political declamation in Dryden's heroic drama is anything

more than plastered decoration. . . . In an earlier chapter we have
hesitated to impute to Dryden an adherence to the philosophical conception of determinism which is so frequently debated in his plays. It is likewise neither necessary nor advisable to take his characters literally as his
mouthpieces on political theory.[18]

Defining the concept of absolute monarchy, Bredvold rightly says,
"What the doctrine really meant in the time of Dryden was that
there must be in government an ultimate authority beyond which
there can be no appeal. When that authority has spoken,
it cannot be impugned or brought to trial for its decision without
crumbling the fabric of government." [19]

Dryden was then a man who, through a skepticism natural to
his temperament and present in the age, was eventually led on
to Catholicism in religion and Toryism in politics. The conclusions
we have reached regarding Dryden's hero do not contradict this
portrait, but, on the contrary, support it.

Bredvold says: "That Dryden, true to the traditions of skepticism,
shared this distrust of human nature [Montaigne's distrust] is
obvious to the most cursory reader of his political poems." [20] This
should also be obvious to the reader of the heroic plays. As we
have seen, the hero is to shun his passions and obey reason, but
this reason is a set of rules which society imposes on him. Responsibility is shifted from the individual to society; Dryden not only
distrusts the individual's natural impulses, but he does not even
trust his reason.

In a recent article, J. A. Winterbottom stresses the predominance
of Stoic philosophy in Dryden's tragedies. He notes the interest and
admiration which Stoicism had commanded in England for over
a hundred years, and Dryden's own praise of the virtues of humilia-
tion, resignation, and contempt for the world. Though Winterbottom
acknowledges that these virtues are as much Christian as Stoic,
he nevertheless finds that Dryden's tragedies are a showplace for
Stoic philosophy.[21] His arguments are interesting and in some instances convincing; yet on the whole his stand must be rejected.
To illustrate his point, he says of Montezuma in *The Indian Emperor,*
"yet even so abandoned a character as Montezuma is capable of
flashes of Stoical behavior." [22] The word "flashes" is right since the
overall impression which Montezuma conveys is one of abandon
to one's passions rather than of Stoical restraint. Winterbottom
next takes up Maximin:

In *Tyrannick Love* . . . appears the Emperor Maximin, Dryden's first fully developed Marlovian hero. With his monstrous desires, his ruthless treatment of those who oppose him, and his addiction to rant, he is in every way the counterpart of Tamburlaine. His character is, of course, unalloyed by any hint of Stoicism, but like other writers of heroic trage- dies, Dryden indicates his disapproval of the heroic personality by plac- ing it in a context which includes some elements of that philosophy.[23]

Much of what is quoted here has more or less been answered in the body of this study: Maximin is not "in every way a counter- part of Tamburlaine." How can he be if Tamburlaine is all will and Maximin has none? On the other hand, Dryden's "disapproval of the heroic personality" is a phrase that needs clarification. The object of this study was partly to arrive at a definition of the heroic temper. My conclusion, based on the plays considered as drama and action and not as a rostrum for diverse opinions, was that the hero obeys reason, curbs his passions, and denies himself for the good of society.

This picture does not contradict the innumerable instances in which Dryden states that the hero is to be imitated and admired. To have Dryden disapprove of the heroical temper would be to go counter to the all-powerful neoclassical concept of the utilitar- ian end of art. We are all familiar with the process by which the Aristotelian concept of catharsis, through Horace, was transformed by fifteenth and sixteenth century Italian commentators into the "teach and delight" theory which, from Sidney down, was held as an absolute rule by the Renaissance and the neoclassical move- ment.[24] The main new element brought in by this transformation was the notion of admiration and its corollary, poetic justice. A hero is to be admired in order to prompt imitation. If he is to be admired, he has to be virtuous; if virtuous, how can he be punished? This is one of the reasons why we cannot accept Maximin as the hero of *Tyrannic Love*.

The perfection of such stage characters consists chiefly in their likeness to the deficient faulty nature, which is their original; only . . . in such cases . . . there will always be found a better likeness and a worse, and the better is constantly to be chosen; I mean in tragedy, which represents the figures of the highest form among mankind. . . . Tis true that all manner of imperfections must not be taken away from the characters; and the reason is that there may be left some grounds of pity for their misfortunes; wicked they would be hated, saintly, their misery would bring on accusation of injustice against heaven. . . . Thus in a tragedy

. . . the hero of the piece must be advanced foremost to the view of the reader, or the spectator: he must outshine the rest of all the characters; he must appear the prince of them, like the sun in the Copernican system, encompassed with the less noble planets.[25]

In Dryden's hand, the Aristotelian notion of the tragic flaw becomes merely "specks of frailty and deficiency." [26] Had there been no alternative to Maximin, we would have had to admit that Dryden does the contrary of what he preaches; but we have already seen how Porphyrius is in every way a hero to be admired, what we call a "heroical" hero. It is only if one insists on calling Maximin "heroic" that one may conclude that Dryden disapproved of "heroic" heroes. It seems more logical to assume that the "heroic" is something different from and opposed to Maximin. Consequently, the Stoicism which Winterbottom sees reflected in the evolution of the hero from the Montezuma-Maximin type, to the Aureng-Zebe type (Almanzor being the turning point) does not exist according to our premises: the Montezuma of *The Indian Emperor* is the prototype of the emperor in *Aureng-Zebe*, and Maximin is Nourmahal's alter ego.

Speaking of the tragedy, Winterbottom contends that "in Dryden's hands the genre actually became a means of subtly negating the very force which gave it life. The heroic temperament is gradually trimmed and finally tamed, and the Marlovian hero who had looked on the community variously as slaves, victims, and spectators, finally accepts it as an object worthy of his devotion." [27]

I believe, on the contrary, that the heroic temperament was not gradually trimmed, for it never needed trimming in the first place since Cortez, Guyomar, and Porphyrius belong to Dryden's very first heroic tragedies and were prototypes repeated in Almanzor and Aureng-Zebe. The "heroic" hero was never essentially Marlovian and did not "finally" accept the community as an object of devotion but had done so from the beginning (Cortez, Guyomar, Porphyrius). The essential difference between my point of view and Winterbottom's may be more readily understood when he says that Dryden "assumed that the passions, though powerful, can be controlled. This assumption in itself did much to shatter the mystique surrounding the hero whose passions were usually considered to be irresistible." [28] My conclusion is that no heroic play of Dryden contends that the hero's passions are irresistible, but that on the contrary a hero is a hero only to the extent that he controls his passions.

Winterbottom explains that Dryden reverted to Stoicism because he felt that "ancient articles of faith" (sense of honor, bond between father and child, duties of obedience on the part of the subject, of solicitude on the part of the ruler) "could no longer be accepted without question," and that Dryden "seemed unable to give himself wholly to either conservative or liberal thought." [29] I have tried to show that in the heroic plays Dryden was completely won over to conservatism. Winterbottom asks: "Within the tragedies, then, what code of behavior could be offered both for the able individual who was quite prepared to violate sanctified social and political forms in his quest for power and for the weaker individuals who merely suffered amid the contention for power?" [30] His answer is Stoicism. However, in both the types he describes, we do not recognize our hero, as we see him in the plays; the individual prepared to "violate sanctified social and political forms in his quest for power" is not the hero but the antihero, that is, the villain. But even if we disregard the plays, Stoicism as such does not fit in with Dryden's skepticism. Essentially, Stoicism is dogmatic and optimistic.

Throughout his study, *Stoics and Skeptics,* Edwyn Bevan implies that whenever Stoicism took the upper hand as a philosophical system, it did so as a reaction to skepticism: "Stoicism, as it appears to me, was a system put together hastily, violently, to meet a desperate emergency," this emergency being "the skepticism which had become general in the Greek schools with the activity of speculation and the Sophistic movement." The doctrine of certainty in Stoicism, met the need "to give a complete answer to the enigma of the universe, compact in all its parts, since nothing which left any room for doubt to get in could give a bewildered world security and guidance. . . . It was for the faith in Providence above all else that the Stoic stood in the ancient world." [31] "The Stoics attempted to frame a theory of the physical universe, of the individual man as he finds himself under compulsion in this universe and, combining the two, to formulate a rule of life in conformity with Reason," says R. M. Wenley.[32] We can see by this definition how Stoicism could be mistaken for the trends in Dryden's plays. But the dogma, the certainty, the explanatory content of Stoicism are what make it improbable as a framework for these plays. To cite Wenley again: "Given a dumb and deaf deity, the theory [Stoicism] ends in apotheosis of personal reason, and each individual becomes his own God." [33] Here we recognize neither Dryden nor the "heroic" hero.

Rather than identify the virtues of humility, resignation, and contempt for the world with Stoicism, we would prefer to give them their Christian connotation. It is from this angle that an evaluation of the hero is offered here. This is a very subjective interpretation, but it seems logical, if the conclusions arrived at in the preceding chapters have any validity. In the light of these conclusions, the quality of the hero which appears to be the most striking is that of self-denial. One of Dryden's definitions of a hero includes "piety to the Gods and a dutiful affection to his father, love to his relations, care of his people, courage and conduct in the wars, gratitude to those who had obliged him, and justice in general to mankind." [34] We have here the portrait of a hero in what we may call his "positive" aspect: what he does or is supposed to do. The other side of this "positive" is what interests us here, and the heroic tragedies throw more light on that other side than does Dryden's definition. This definition shows the hero performing his duties toward others; the tragedies show him also as denying himself everything. This denial of the self is what makes of the hero not just a Stoic, not just a Christian, but mainly a Roman Catholic Christian. The Stoic relies on himself. So ultimately does the Protestant since he finds his God in himself or through himself. But the Roman Catholic Christian exercises the virtues of humility and resignation in order to deliver himself up wholly and completely to authority (the authority of the church).

To stretch this point would be awkward and unjustified. The "heroic" hero is, of course, not a "Catholic" hero, and Dryden would no doubt be astonished to hear him qualified as such. The only validity of such an evaluation resides in the sense of completeness it gives to conclusions already reached. In view of Dryden's ultimate conversion to Catholicism, it seems pertinent to note that already in the heroic tragedies, his heroes reflect Roman Catholic ideology. This fact tends to undermine such statements as "the heroic play of Dryden is essentially a naturalistic and in part a romantic revolt against Christian humanism"—which in another part of the same essay is defined as emphasizing "man's rationality and his control of the passions." [35]

CHAPTER 5

THE HERO IN DRYDEN'S
OTHER SERIOUS PLOTS

As POINTED OUT at the beginning of Chapter 2, the present body
of criticism on Dryden's dramatic work seems to set a line of de-
marcation between the plays we have examined in the preceding
chapters and the rest of Dryden's serious plays. Exactly how these
other plays differ from the heroic plays is not made very clear.
However, they are never referred to as "heroic plays" but as "tragedies." The heroic play is said to have culminated in *The Conquest
of Granada*. Speaking of the heroic play as a literary genre, Alan
McKillop believes that "the movement dies down in the late 1670's,
but leaves a legacy of turgidity and rant to later English tragedy.
The heroic play may be described as a deliberate attempt to be
romantic and heroic in an unromantic and unheroic age, an age that
was drawing a sharp line between imagination and reason." [1] *All
for Love* is commonly assumed to be a "turning point," a rejection of
the heroic genre, a "return to Shakespeare," whatever that may
mean. Dobrée, in his *Restoration Tragedy*, minutely analyzes *All for
Love* in a separate chapter from the one he devotes to Dryden, and
seems to consider this play Dryden's "masterpiece"—not only
superior to but different from the rest of his dramatic works.
Pendlebury's opinion is that in this play Dryden "rejected at once
the fetters of rhyme and the heroic conception of the drama. Dryden's example being followed in a short time by Otway, the heroic
play disappeared from the English stage." [2] "When in *All for Love*
(1678)," says G. H. Nettleton, "he [Dryden] turned to blank verse
and a Shakespearean theme, rhymed heroic drama has had its day

50

and practically ceased to be." [3] Margaret Sherwood, who analyzes in three successive chapters Dryden's comedies, heroic plays, and tragedies, places *All for Love* among the tragedies. Cecil V. Deane stresses the point that the heroic play is actually a phenomenon occurring over a very short span of time.[4] More recent criticism does not change this picture appreciably.

It is clear then that Dryden wrote different kinds of tragedy: the heroic plays, the tragedies proper, and the serious plots of his tragicomedies.[5] Our purpose is not, of course, to prove that the tragedies are heroic plays. However, in this study of Dryden's heroic plays we have examined the heroic hero and arrived at a certain definite characterization which is repeated over and over in these plays. My contention is that if we now turn to Dryden's tragedies and the serious plots of the tragicomedies, we shall find that the hero in these plays displays essentially the same basic character as in the heroic plays. There are the same motivations, the same scale of values, the same conception of character—in a word, the same "type" as in the heroic plays. To put it differently, Dryden's hero in the heroic plays is also the hero in his other serious plays. There may be a slight shift in emphasis; the character may be approached and treated from a different point of view; but essentially we are confronted in all of Dryden's serious plots with the same basic characterization of the principal hero.

Some of Dryden's plays have no literary value whatsoever and are frankly unreadable—*Amboyna,* for instance. These plays will not be studied in this section. It would also be exceedingly repetitious to examine thoroughly all the better plays. After considering *All for Love,* it will be necessary to dwell on only one tragicomedy, one later tragedy, and to glance briefly at some of the other plays which present some interest.

All for Love deserves to be studied first, if only because critics find it so different from what preceded.[6] Antony, beaten at Actium, has shut himself up and refuses to see anyone, including Cleopatra. Ventidius, one of his old generals, has come to Alexandria and insists on seeing him. Even his enemies acknowledge Ventidius' worth:

ALEXAS: A mortal foe he was to us, and Egypt.
           But, let me witness to the worth I hate
           A braver Roman never drew a Sword;
           Firm to his Prince, but as a friend, not slave.

> He ne'r was of his pleasures; but presides
> O'er all his cooler hours and morning counsels:
> In short, the plainness, fierceness, rugged virtue
> Of an old true-stampt Roman lives in him."
>
> (I,i)

When told of Antony's mood, Ventidius recognizes a familiar pattern of behavior:

>   Just, just his nature.
> Virtues' his path; but sometimes 'tis too narrow
> For his vast Soul; and then he starts out wide,
> And bounds into a Vice that bears him far
> From his first course, and plunges him in ills:
> But when his danger makes him find his fault,
> Quick to observe, and full of sharp remorse,
> He censures eagerly his own misdeeds,
> Judging himself with malice to himself,
> And not forgiving what as Man he did,
> Because his other parts are more than Man.—
> He must not thus be lost.
>
> (I,i)

In this description it is not hard to recognize our hero. Antony is essentially virtuous, but he has a "vast soul." Ventidius is definitely not praising this vastness of the soul since it is what leads Antony "into a vice that bears him far / From his first course." Antony has the awareness we have found in all of Dryden's heroes: he knows what is right and what is wrong: "Quick to observe, and full of sharp remorse, / He censures eagerly his own misdeeds." Antony is cut from the pattern of the heroic heroes; there is nothing Aristotelian or Shakespearean about him. He is not a great man brought to his downfall by a tragic flaw to which he is blind. Lear is great because he has a vast soul, the very quality which is a failing in Antony, but he is not virtuous. The most important difference, however, is the awareness which Antony has and which Lear lacks: Lear would be incapable, at the start of the play, of comprehending his eventual downfall, even if he were able to see the events that lead to it projected on a screen. This awareness or consciousness, is the very thing into which he grows all through the play and which makes of him every inch a king. The nature of that awareness is, of course, not the same in both these characters; as we shall see, Antony's is an *a priori* knowledge of dicta and rules for conduct which make it easy for him to give a value judgment.

If an act is in accordance with these rules, it is right; if not, it is wrong. The awareness Lear gains has nothing to do with an external scale of values; it is something that is bred in him through a destructive process of awakening which actually leaves him raving mad: all the familiar and reliable landmarks have to be torn down before they are replaced by a different scale of values inborn and inbred. It is characteristic that he is described as "every inch a King" when he walks mad on the shore, but it is a perfectly fitting moment since he is then the living proof of the conflict he has resolved in himself.

Another aspect which differentiates these two types of awareness is that since Antony's is an external one, it is absolute and unchangeable, and yields judgments in either black or white. But Lear's never ceases to grow. There is no one precise moment at which Lear gains knowledge of what is right or wrong, as such, and can tell himself: "From now on, I know what to do." On the contrary, the more his personality broadens, the less he feels he knows; he actually becomes aware of knowing nothing. The greater he becomes, the less dogmatic he is. His last words are still words of bewilderment: "Why should a dog, a horse, a rat, have life, / And thou no breath at all?" [7]

But neoclassicism did not ask questions it could not answer; it had devised a pattern of answers and asked only the questions which fitted into that pattern. The notion of poetic justice seems to have been evolved precisely in that context: retribution must follow crime, but it should be scaled to that crime. In a perfectly ordered world, villains are punished and the good are rewarded; when the good manifest what Dryden calls "frailty," they are punished, too, but never in excess of what their crime deserves.

In his preface to *All for Love* Dryden says he chose his subject because of the "excellency of the Moral. For the chief persons represented, were famous patterns of unlawful love; and their end accordingly was unfortunate. All reasonable men have long since concluded, that the Heroe of the Poem ought not to be a character of perfect Virtue, for, then, he could not without injustice, be made unhappy; nor yet altogether wicked, because he could not then be pitied." [8] Most of all, the rule of poetic justice applies to the innocent since as Dryden says in his essay, "Of Poetry and Painting," if a perfect character is punished, "his or her misfortunes would produce impious thoughts in the beholders; they would accuse the heavens of injustice. . . ." [9] When the neoclassicists married Cordelia off to

Edgar, they were not just trying to please the larger public; the whole concept of an innocent punished for crimes he did not commit was incomprehensible to them. It destroyed their whole well-organized world. Cordelia's death was unnecessary, and so was Lear's. After all, the man had only made out of rashness a mistake in judgment and had been adequately punished for it. Why kill him off along with his poor innocent lovely daughter? But then, what could one expect of the Elizabethans?—"when men were dull, and conversations low. . . . If love and honour now are higher raised / 'Tis not the poet, but the age is praised," says Dryden.[10] Shakespeare's age was "an age less polished, more unskilled" and could not be expected to understand the niceties of poetic justice and decorum.[11] A civilized age owes it to itself to delight only in violence sanctioned by moral laws, and not in violence for its own sake.

In Shakespeare's case, Thomas Rymer's judgments are notoriously "infamous." Yet, Rymer undoubtedly was representative of his age. He just happened to be that rare phenomenon, a spectator completely impervious to Shakespeare. Yet the basic principles on which he opposed him are those of his age. Rymer's analysis of *Othello*, a masterpiece in its own way, is enlightening. The first thing he looks for is the "Moral," and this he seems to find difficult to pinpoint. Whether tongue-in-cheek or not, he summarizes the different possibilities: "First, this may be a caution to all Maidens of Quality how, without their Parents consent, they run away with Blackamoors. . . . Secondly, this may be a warning to all good Wives, that they look well to their Linnen. . . . Thirdly, this may be a lesson to Husbands, that before their Jealousie be Tragical, the proofs may be Mathematical." [12] Evidently, Rymer has completely missed whatever *Othello* has to give. Why? What strikes Rymer most are what he calls the improbabilities. The mechanical logical errors of the play are not in question here, though he dwells on them at some length. What seems to upset him is that things are not what one would expect them to be. How can Desdemona fall in love with a "negro"? "All this is very strange. And therefore pleases such as reflect not on the improbability. This match may well be without the parents Consent. . . . The Characters or Manners, which are the second part in a Tragedy, are not less unnatural and improper, than the Fable was improbable and absurd." [13] Rymer is bothered most by the character of Iago. Iago is a soldier; everyone knows what a soldier is or should be; so does Shakespeare, "but to entertain the

Audience with something new and surprising, against common sense, and Nature, he would pass upon us a close, dissembling, false, insinuating rascal, instead of an open-hearted, frank, plain dealing Souldier, a character constantly worn by them for some thousands of years in the World." [14] This need for the common, the familiar, the expected—the yearning for rules which are a haven where one can find security belong to the very spiritual climate in which the hero of the heroic play felt at home. That same climate could only breed the concept of poetic justice. Given his own ideology, poor Rymer is understandably puzzled:

Rather may we ask here what unatural [sic] crime Desdemona, or her parents had committed, to bring his judgment, down upon her; to Wed a Black-amoor, and innocent to be thus cruelly murdered by him. What instruction can we make out of this catastrophe? Or whither must our reflection lead us? Is not this to envenome and sour our spirits, to make us repine and grumble at Providence; and the government of the World? If this be our end, what boots it to be Virtuous? [15]

This same principle of poetic justice applies in Antony's case. Antony's end is tragic; consequently, he should be guilty; guilt can only be assumed when knowledge is present; hence Antony is not blind to his own nature as Othello is. He knows his crime, what he has to pay for it, and why he committed it. Dryden, in the preface to the play, makes this point very clear: ". . . For the crimes of love which they both committed, were not occasion'd by any necessity, or fatal ignorance, but were wholly voluntary; since our passions are, or ought to be, within our power." [16] In the very first scene where Antony and Ventidius fall tearfully into each other's arms, Antony confesses: "But I have lost my Reason, have disgrac'd / The name of Soldier with inglorious ease" (I,i). When he asks Ventidius to curse him, the latter refuses because "You are too sensible already / Of what you've done, too conscious of your failings" (I,i). When Ventidius blames Cleopatra, the friends quarrel but Antony quickly acknowledges that deep inside he feels likewise: "Pr'y thee, forgive me. / Why did'st thou tempt my anger, by discovery / Of what I would not hear"? The scene which ends the first act has Antony pledge to reform: "Thy praises were unjust; but, I'll deserve them, / And yet mend all. Do with me what thou wilt. . . ." He will leave Cleopatra "Though Heaven knows I love / Beyond Life, Conquest, Empire; all but Honor." This resolution draws Ventidius's commendation: "Methinks you breathe / Another Soul; Your looks

are more Divine; / You Speak a hero; and you move a God" (I,i).
It is interesting to pause for a moment at the end of this first act
and consider the play from the point of view of technical play-
writing. The most important feature of this play is that the plot or
story or what Dryden calls the "fable," is well known. The "what
happens" question is already answered as far as the spectator is
concerned: Antony is not going to shake off his fascination for
Cleopatra, and both lovers are going to die. The type of suspense
lacking here is certainly not necessary to a play since the "how does
it happen" can be a more interesting problem. The "how" question
itself can be considered from at least two points of view: the obvious
one involving external events, which can be of little interest since
the end is known, and the one that involves a study of what goes on
inside a character—his motivations, his whole conscious and unconscious psychological portrait. This analysis is valid in that by seeing "how" a character acts, we understand "why" he acts the way he
does. In the case of Antony, after the very first scene in which we
are introduced to him and which ends the first act, we are in
possession of all the elements that tell us the reason why he is going
to end the way he does, even before we have been shown how it
happens. Antony knows perfectly well what he is supposed to do,
what he wants to do, how to do it, and why he may not do it. So does
the spectator, who, as a matter of fact, has one advantage over
Antony: if Antony knows why he may not do it, the spectator knows
why he does not do it, since he is cognizant of the denouement.

Consequently, *All for Love* does not even generate the kind of
suspense typical of lesser known plots. When Almanzor oscillates
between his weaker and stronger self, the spectator can still wonder
which one is going to win. But in spite of the fact that his oscillation
is completely without interest as dramatic action in this play, it is
precisely what we get in *All for Love*. In Act I Antony decides to
leave Cleopatra; at the end of Act II, he will stay with her.

> I'm eager to return before I go;
> For, all the pleasures I have known, beat thick
> On my remembrance: How I long for night!
> That both the sweets of mutual love may try,
> And once Triumph o'er Caesar ere we dye.
> (II, i)

Antony's last words in Act III, addressed to Octavia who has come
to fetch him away, are:

This is thy Triumph
Lead me where thou wilt,
Ev'n to thy Brother's Camp.
(III,i)

In Act IV, Antony is not lured back by Cleopatra's charms, but the result is the same. Misled by Ventidius and Alexas, he thinks Cleopatra is false to him with his friend Dolabella; he cannot control his passion, and his jealousy irritates Octavia, who leaves him.

ANTONY: Why was I fram'd with this plain, honest heart,
    Which knows not to disguise its griefs and weakness,
    But bears its workings outward to the World?
(IV,i)

Evidently, he wishes Octavia had not left him. Now that he has nothing to hope for from Octavius, he can only stay and fight him.

The action in Act V is the familiar one. Beaten and believing Cleopatra dead, Antony falls on his sword. Cleopatra reaches him in time for both of them to acknowledge their love.

This pendulum movement which Dryden apparently mistakes for Aristotle's *peripeteia* is actually the only possible one, given the characterization. When everything is pushed to its extreme implication at the start, there is nowhere to go from that extreme point but to return to where one has started from.

One other characteristic of *All for Love* seems to evolve directly from that very same set characterization which we have found to be identical to that of the heroic play. Since the hero can or should act only according to a given pattern, the theatrical interest, in the heroic plays, resides in an accumulation of events, of climaxes following close one upon another.

In *All for Love*, because Dryden wanted to write a classical play in the strictest sense, and because he was limited by his subject, the interest had to be of a different nature, that is, sentimental. The "terror" element is lost in favor of the "pity" element. This may be one of the major differences between the heroic plays and *All for Love*. The characterization is the same, but because passion does not overcome reason, because of the subsequent denouement, the pathetic takes the upper hand since something has to be done to get the spectator emotionally involved. For sheer tear-jerking sentimentality, *All for Love* can compete with the best (or possibly worst) of the sentimental plays of the eighteenth century. Here are a few passages picked at random:

VENTIDIUS: (*weeping*): Look, Emperor, this is no common dew,
  I have not wept this Forty years; but now
  My Mother comes afresh into my eyes;
  I cannot help her softness.
ANTONY: By Heav'n, he weeps! poor, good
  Old man he weeps!
  The big round drops course one another down
  The furrows of his cheeks. Stop them. . . .
VENTIDIUS: I'll do my best.
ANTONY: Sure there's contagion in the tears of Friends:
  See, I have caught it too. Believe me, 'tis not
  For my own griefs, but thine. Nay, father!
VENTIDIUS: Emperor!

                                      (I,i)

CLEOPATRA: Now, what news my Charmion?
  Will he be kind? And will he not forsake me?
  Am I to live, or dye? nay, Do I live?
  Or am I dead?

                                      (II,i)

CLEOPATRA: Go; leave me, Soldier.
  (For you're no more a Lover), leave me dying;
  Push me all pale and panting from your bosom.

                                      (II,i)

When Octavia tries to win Antony back, she pushes her children toward him:

OCTAVIA: . . . Go, I say, and pull him to me,
  And pull him to yourselves from that bad Woman.
  You, Agrippina, hang upon his arms.
  And you, Antonia, clasp about his waist.
  If he will shake you off, if he will dash you
  Against the Pavement, you must bear it, Children,
  For you are mine, and I was born to suffer.
           (*Here the Children go to him.*)
VENTIDIUS: Was ever sight so moving?
  Emperor!
DOLABELLA: Friend!
OCTAVIA: Husband!
BOTH CHILDREN: Father!
ANTONY: I am vanquished. Take me,
  Octavia, take me, Children; share me all. (*Embracing them*)
                                    (III, i)

As for Cleopatra, she begs for pity throughout the play. She is presented as a poor lovely soul, made the toy of circumstances. Apparently she had been virtually raped by Caesar:

He first possess'd my person; you my Love.
Caesar lov'd me, but I lov'd Antony.
If I endured him after 'twas because
I judg'd it due to the first name of Men,
And, half constrain'd, I gave as to a Tyrant
What he would take by force.

(II,i)

Insulted by Octavia's, "Shame of our sex, / Dost thou not blush to own those black endearments / That make sin pleasing?" Cleopatra does not rise above whimpering:

. . . The World condemns poor me;
For I have lost my Honour, lost my Fame,
And stained the glory of my Royal House,
And all to bear the branded Name of Mistress.

(III,i)

She confides to Alexas:

. . . Nature meant me
A Wife, a silly harmless household Dove,
Fond without art; and kind without deceit;
But Fortune, that has made a Mistress of me,
Has thrust me out to the wide world, unfurnish'd
Of falsehood to be happy.

(IV, i)

This transformation of Cleopatra into a middle class bourgeois housewife is not just a question of taste; otherwise, one would never forgive Dryden for having attempted it. It is hard to believe that simply for lack of taste, whole generations would cry at Cleopatra's fate and breathe more freely when Cordelia and Edgar go on to live happily ever after. It can only be because ideologically they are attuned to what they are offered. And the ideology of *All for Love* is the same as what we have found in the heroic tragedy.

In *The Spanish Friar* Leonora is Queen of Aragon only because her father has usurped the crown by deposing the lawful king and murdering his children.[17] Aragon is besieged by Abdalla the Moor and his forces. Leonora's father had promised her hand to Bertran, whose own father had helped him in deposing the lawful king. The Spanish are in a desperate situation when Torrismond, a Spanish general with meager forces, beats off the Moors. Bertran, who is jealous of him, nevertheless offers congratulations, but Torrismond claims that he has acted only out of honor and not to win praise:

> . . . But let Honour
> Call for my Bloud; and sluce it into streams;
> Turn Fortune loose again to my pursuit;
> And let me hunt her through embattell'd Foes,
> In dusty Plains, amidst the Cannons roar,
> There will I be the first.
>
> (I, i)

Learning of Bertran's plans to marry Leonora, Torrismond cannot hide his pain and discloses his love for her. However, aware of his lowly station, he does not nourish any hope of attaining her.

> Heav'n may be thought on, though too high to climbe.
> . . . Queens may be lov'd,
> And so may Gods; else, why are Altars rais'd?
> Why shines the Sun, but that he may be view'd?
> But, Oh! when he's too bright, if then we gaze
> 'Tis but to weep; and close our eyes in darkness.
>
> (I, i)

Bertran, understandably, is far from being pleased. When Torrismond is insolent with Bertran, the Queen, hearing of the quarrel, summons Torrismond to her. There, he immediately loses all bravura: "Like a led Victim, to my Death I'll goe; / And, dying, bless the hand that gave the blow" (II,i).

Apparently, Leonora does not know Torrismond very well since he has always been fighting away from the court. She is surprised by his gentle countenance:

> But where's the Fierceness, the Disdainful Pride;
> The Haughty Port, the Fiery Arrogance?
> By all these Marks, this is not sure the man.

During the interview the Queen falls in love with Torrismond:

> A change so swift, what heart did ever feel!
> It rush'd upon me, like a mighty Stream,
> And bore me in a moment far from Shore.
> I've lov'd away my self; in one short hour
> Already am I gone an Age of Passion.
>
> (II, i)

She manages a private meeting with him and upbraids Torrismond for presuming to love her. He protests that his love cannot hurt her since he loves in vain: "Good Heav'ns, why gave you me a Monarch's Soul, / And crusted it with base Plebeian Clay!" (II,i) The Queen, however, relents and offering him her pity, bids him hope. Torrismond is elated.

Leonora, completely overpowered by her love for Torrismond, tries to arouse Bertran's jealousy in order to gain grounds to reject him, but he sees the snare and is not provoked. As a last resort she explains that she put off their marriage because she is frightened by her people, who resent Bertran. He advises her to have the rightful, imprisoned king murdered. She refuses at first, but on second thought decides that by doing so she would make her crown more secure for Torrismond. She does not command Bertran to do anything, but tells him, "I leave it all to you; think what you doe, / You doe for him I love" (III,i).

After Bertran leaves, Torrismond enters and begs the Queen, who is by now his avowed lover, to have pity on the King, whom he has just visited in prison. When Leonora tells him of Bertran's plans to murder him, Torrismond is horrified and pleads with her, showing the extent of her crime. She relents: "I knew this Truth, but I repell'd that thought." She is sending for Bertran when she receives his message: " 'Tis performed."

TORRISMOND: Ten thousand Plagues consume him, Furies drag him,
  Fiends tear him; Blasted be the Arm that strook,
  The Tongue that order'd;—Onely She be spar'd
  That hindred not the deed. . . .

                                      (III,i)

He is beside himself with pain. But Leonora begs him to forget: Bertran's act gives her an opportunity to reject him, and that same night she plans to wed Torrismond in secret. In spite of a gloomy presentiment, Torrismond accepts.

Raymond, Torrismond's father, has come back to court and witnesses Leonora's rejection of Bertran on the grounds that he committed a base murder. Raymond's allegiance is to the old king, and he seems crushed when Leonora confides to him that she loves Torrismond. When he sees Torrismond next, he tries to rouse him against Leonora. But Torrismond will not be moved:

TORRISMOND: How cou'd my Hand rebell against my Heart?
RAYMOND: How could your Heart rebell against your Reason?
TORRISMOND: No Honour bids me fight against my self:
  The Royal Family is all extinct,
  And she who reigns bestows her Crown on me.

But Raymond urges him to avenge the death of the King, for that King was Torrismond's real father, and Torrismond is his lawful heir. Torrismond, however, is appalled, since he has already married

Leonora: "Th' Usurper of my Throne, my House's Ruin, / The Murtherer of my Father, is my Wife!" (IV,i) Torrismond knows no peace:

> Love, Justice, Nature, Pity, and Revenge
> Have kindled up a wild-fire in my Breast
> And I am all a Civil-war within!

He cannot make himself face Leonora:

> Oh! That I could with Honour love her more,
> Or hate her less with Reason! See, she weeps;
> Thinks me unkind, or false, and knows not why
> I thus estrange my person from her Bed.

Torrismond, under Leonora's prodding, finally discloses his true identity. But when he learns that Raymond has roused the people against Leonora, he decides to protect her and declares himself the true king (V,i). But Raymond, though beaten, insists on seeing justice done to Leonora. Torrismond's heart is breaking with pain, but he admits this should be done; Leonora, however, has already decided to leave him and to spend the rest of her life repenting of her crime in a convent. She shows such deep remorse that even Raymond is moved. But everything ends happily since Bertran discloses that, having guessed Leonora's intent, he has outwitted her by not murdering the King and only spreading the rumor of his death. Torrismond declares: "O Bertran, O! No more my Foe but, brother: / One act like this blots out a thousand Crimes." Since Leonora is innocent, she and Torrismond presumably go on to live happily ever after (V,i).

Torrismond is brave, wins battles single-handed, and is devoted to honor. Though an ardent lover, he does not presume to fulfill his love since it would be improper for a commoner to marry a queen. (Let us remember that this was Montezuma's "frailty" in *The Indian Queen*.) It is evident that with very few changes, Torrismond could just as well be the hero in a heroic play.

From the point of view of ideology, the question of responsibility and guilt in this play presents some interest. Torrismond feels he is bound by honor to revenge his father on Leonora, though he feels he cannot do it because she is his wife. He still loves her, yet he feels revulsion toward her and cannot share her bed—all this because she contributed to the murder of his father. Yet, he knew of the murder when he married her; what he did not know was that the supposedly murdered man was his father. Consequently, when he shrinks from her, it is not because she is a criminal as such, but because a whole code of honor imposes on him duties that conflict with his love for her. It is quite understandable, of course, to feel more revulsion for a crime perpetrated against your own father than against a stranger. But in Torrismond's case, the disproportion between his attitude towards Leonora, before and after he learns the real identity of the murdered man, is quite relevant, especially since all his life Torrismond had loved Raymond as a father, and had deeply respected the King. Though Leonora is guilty of murdering a king and a great man, Torrismond can love her and feels free to respect her; the minute the murdered one is revealed as his father—that is, a person Torrismond has never known as such—his whole world crumbles.

There are suggestions that an act was judged only or rather mainly in its social rather than in its personal context. For instance, there is no doubt whatsoever in the mind of all those concerned that Leonora is guilty of murder. Yet when the victim escapes his fate because of external circumstances, she is immediately cleared of all dishonor. The fact that she had willed the murder, that the intended victim was her father-in-law, completely disappears from the picture; since the King did not die, she is not guilty.

The situation is the same with Bertran: "One act like this blots out a thousand crimes," says Torrismond as he embraces him. Actually, this act is nothing more than a further villainy on the part of Bertran. He had goaded the Queen into willing the murder, and yet he had betrayed her and disobeyed her orders, purely out of personal egotistical motives. But once again, we have the proof that motives and motivations were not what interested authors and spectators. An act was judged according to its consequences. "Why" something happens was ignored in favor of "what" happens. The social emphasis in this type of interest is obvious; instead of looking into himself, a character prefers looking outside at the world. An act is judged not in its relation to the individual but in its relation to society. An external scale of values is applied as opposed to an internal one.

In *Cleomenes*, the ex-king of Sparta has taken refuge at the Egyptian court, which is ruled by the weak, luxurious Ptolomy and his mistress, Cassandra.[18] There he awaits the help Ptolomy has

promised him, in his attempt to reconquer Sparta. Cleomenes knows
his own worth:

> Ah! why ye Gods, must Cleomenes wait
> On this Effeminate Luxurious Court,
> For tardy helps of base Egyptian Bands?
> Why have not I, whose individual mind
> Would ask a Nation of such Souls t'inform it,
> Why have not I ten Thousand hands to fight
> It all my self? and make the Work my own?
>
> (I,i)

Cassandra, as was predictable, falls in love with Cleomenes. We
immediately recognize the pattern of the villain heroine in the
heroic play; she is completely dominated by her passion which, as
we would expect, is of a low, physical nature:

> . . . When we are a thirst,
> Or hungry, Will imperious Nature stay?
> Not Eat nor Drink, before 'tis bid, fall on. . . .
>
> (II,i)

She tries to make her love plain to Cleomenes by inviting him to
ponder over a painting representing the rape of Helen by Paris. The
judgment of Cleomenes is unequivocal:

> A base dishonest Act; to violate
> All Hospitable Rites, to force away,
> His Benefactors Wife; Ungrateful Villain;
> And so the Gods, Th' avenging Gods have judg'd.
>
> (II,ii)

Throughout the play we see in Cleomenes an awareness of the
proper way to act under various exterior pressures. For instance,
when thrown into prison with his wife, child, and mother—apparently betrayed by his only friend—Cleomenes repudiates the suggestion of his mother, Cratisclaea, that they all commit suicide:
"Not so, but that we durst not tempt the Gods, / To break their
images without their leave" (IV,i). When they are all faint with
hunger and his son begs him leave to die, "Or give me leave to die—
as I desir'd; / For without your consent, Heaven Knows I dare
not," Cleomenes still does not rebel: "I prithee stay a little; I am
loath / To say hard things of Heaven!" (V,i)

With the help of his Egyptian friend Cleanthes, Cleomenes attempts an uprising. Confronted with Cassandra, Cleanthes wants to
expose her, but Cleomenes stops him:

Peace, Peace, my Friend.
No injuries from Women can provoke
A Man of Honour to expose their Fame.
(V,i)

When one stops to think that this Cassandra was the cause of all his misfortunes, that she had starved him and his family for more than three days, that she would stop at nothing (and she does not) to gain her end, Cleomenes' respect for decorum and propriety is at the very least astonishing to a modern reader. However, it must have been something admirable to Restoration audiences, since obedience to rules and dicta (decorum) was the only reliable standard of conduct.

In this play Cleomenes is not guilty (except for having initially lost a battle); yet he ends tragically. It would seem that the rule of poetic justice is flouted, and actually it is. But when the reader views the tragedy as a whole, he realizes that this is done very carefully. At no time does Cleomenes rebel against his fate. There always seems to be the implication that somewhere, somehow, justice is being done. The blurring of the concept of poetic justice is achieved also by emphasizing pity rather than terror. The spectator is asked to cry over the fate of Cleomenes and his family but is never called upon to identify with them and undergo terror. Though Cleomenes always talks in a manly way, he is revealed in every situation as a passive sufferer. He is continually helpless, and so are his wife, mother, and son, but they never rebel against their fate. So why should the spectator experience a feeling that they themselves do not undergo? When they are all starving, Cleomenes turns to his wife:

CLEOMENES: What! my Cleora?
   I stretch'ed my bounds as far as I could go,
   To shun the sight of what I cannot help;
   A Flow'r withering on the Stalk for want
   Of nourishment from Earth and showers from Heaven:
   All I can give thee is but Rain of Eyes—(*Wiping his eyes*)
CLEORA: Alas! I have not wherewithal to weep:
   My eyes grow dim and stiffen'd up with drought,
   Can hardly rowl and walk their feeble round:
   Indeed—I am faint. . . .
CLEOMENES: How does our helpless Infant?
CLEORA: It wants the Breast, its kindly nourishment:
   And I have none to give from these dry Cesterns,
   Which unsupply'd themselves, can yield no more:

It pull'd and pull'd but now, but nothing came.
At last it drew so hard, that the blood follow'd:
And that Red Milk I found upon its Lips,
Which made me swoon with fear.

(V,i)

Even in death Cleomenes is happy doing what he should. He and his friend Cleanthes decide to run into each other's sword:

CLEOMENES: Then enter We into each others Breasts.
'Tis a sharp passage; yet a kind one too.
But to prevent the blind mistake of Swords,
Lest one drop first, and leave his Friend behind,
Both thrust at once, and home, and at our Hearts:
Let neither stand on Guard, but let our Bosomes
Lie open to each other in our Death,
As in our Life they were—
CLEANTHES: I Seal it thus. (*Kiss and embrace.*)
. . . .
CLEOMENES: . . . Now are you ready, Friend?
CLEANTHES: I am.
CLEOMENES: Then this to our next happy meeting—
   (*They both push together, then stagger backwards
   and fall together in each others Arms.*)
CLEANTHES: Speak, have I serv'd you to your Wish, my Friend?
CLEOMENES: Yes, Friend—thou hast—I have thee in my heart—
   Say—art Thou sped?
CLEANTHES: I am 'tis my last Breath,
CLEOMENES: And mine—Then both are Happy——(*Both die.*)

(V,i)

Indeed, as one character puts it: "So, this was well performed and soon dispatch'd."

It is the same type of emphasis that we find in other plays where poetic justice would apparently be flouted. In *Don Sebastian,* for instance, Sebastian unwittingly marries his own sister.[19] The lovers must part, even though and indeed because they still love each other. But poetic justice intervenes and the play ends on this moral:

And let Sebastian's and Almeyda's Fate,
This dreadful sentence to the World relate,
That unrepented Crimes of Parents dead,
Are justly punish'd on their Childrens head."

(V,i)

"Unrepented" and "justly" are worth noting.

In *Oedipus,* Tiresias is the exponent of the basic notion of justice which neoclassicism offered when events seemed beyond the grasp of rational interpretation, a position which is regularly associated with Alexander Pope who made it famous.[20]

EURYDICE: Is there no God so much a friend to love,
    Who can controle the malice of our fate?
    Are they all deaf? Or have the Gyants Heav'n?
TIRESIAS: The Gods are just—
    But how can Finite measure Infinite?
    Reason! alas, it does not know it self!
    Yet Man, vain Man, wou'd with this short-lin'd Plummet,
    Fathom the vast Abysse of Heav'nly justice.
    What ever is, is in it's causes just;
    Since all things are by Fate. But pur-blind Man
    Sees but a part o' th' Chain; the nearest links;
    His eyes not carrying to that equal Beam
    That poizes all above.

                              (III,i)

This short survey is sufficient to show that characterization and ideology are essentially the same in Dryden's heroic plays and in his other serious plots. Moreover, the concept of poetic justice is equally valid in both types of plays. The essential difference, however, seems to reside in the predominance of the feeling of pity as opposed to admiration which the hero is supposed to awaken in the spectator. The hero of the heroic play is not necessarily more virtuous: Almanzor is certainly less so than Cleomenes. Both these men are made of the same mettle. The only difference between the play with the happy ending and the play with the tragic ending is that in the first, the hero acts on the events, while in the second, he is being acted upon. But whether active or passive, the hero's stand in relation to the events is the same: he neither doubts his own self nor does he doubt the social framework in which he lives. He knows what to do—when, how, and why—even though he could rationally have some ground for doubt (*Don Sebastian, Oedipus*). This awareness, consciousness, certainty are what cause admiration to be replaced by pity. When admiration is no longer paramount and audiences tire of it, only pity can take its place since "virtue" (as understood by neoclassicism) is still the hero's major qualification.

We can see how, far from being a "passing whim," a phenomenon outside the main current of neoclassicism, the heroic tragedy is a necessary link in the English dramatic tradition: after the Jacobean drama with its "romantic" emphasis on terror, the heroic tragedy fosters the feeling of admiration which, in turn, leads directly into the sentimental drama of the eighteenth century with its heavy reliance on pity. As we have seen, in Dryden's own dramatic work we can already begin tracing the latter stage of this evolution.

CHAPTER 6

DRYDEN, CORNEILLE, AND RACINE

AT ONE POINT in this study it seemed pertinent to refer to Corneille and Racine and to associate Dryden more closely with the former than the latter. Both Racine and Corneille are the major exponents of French classical drama, and it is normal to speak of them whenever referring to it. But what often happens when English critics do so is that they seem to make no distinction between Racine and Corneille. Granted that both are neoclassicists, they are nevertheless at opposite poles from each other. To a French critic this is, of course, a truism. La Bruyère's contemporary judgment that "celui-là [Corneille] peint les hommes tels qu'ils devraient être et celui-ci [Racine] tels qu'ils sont," was carried over for generations and is familiar to all French *lycéens* who at one time or another had to treat the subject in a paper. For three hundred years, Corneille, as a playwright, steadily lost ground to Racine. The reason is already endemic in La Bruyère's judgment that Corneille "peint les hommes tels qu'ils devraient être." Although La Bruyère, the moralist, meant to praise Corneille, to say that Corneille paints men the way they should be nevertheless implies that he does not paint them the way they are. To the generations that followed, Corneille gradually came to represent the moralist divorced from reality, as opposed to Racine, the psychological poet whose implacable study of passions left no recess of the human heart unexplored. Running parallel to this trend of criticism was another which stressed the essential moral character of Racine's theater (sin and guilt) as opposed to Corneille's moralizing—amoral if not immoral—drama: Rodrigue is a hero because he kills a man guilty of boxing someone's ears.

The relative merit of Corneille and Racine is a subject which has not yet been settled and never will be since it is directly related to the question of the respective nature of Racine's and Corneille's theater. And this is a domain which will be open to discussion as long as there are critics to discuss it. However, in the light of what has been said concerning Dryden's hero in this study, a *mise au point* will be attempted. The point has already been made in relation to what we have called the historical "moment," when I said that Dryden and Corneille belong to the same tradition, which is not Racine's. We may now proceed to examine a play by Corneille and one by Racine, and compare them to what we know of Dryden's. This may be of particular value since, in the twentieth century, there has been a small but active movement, a sort of renaissance, in favor of Corneille. On the whole, Racine is still the acknowledged great master of French drama, but we shall see that the problem of Corneille's renewed favor with the critics has some points of interest in common with the problems we have had to treat in Dryden. In other words, the conclusions I have reached concerning Dryden's heroic hero may throw some light on the reasons for the renewed interest in Corneille.

The influence of Corneille's criticism on Dryden has been pointed out repeatedly, yet whether one influenced the other or not, they belong to the same dramatic tradition.[1] Corneille has left a short body of criticism which is directly related to his dramatic work; as we know, this is not the case with Dryden. Consequently, it is worth examining Corneille's criticism in relation to the heroic hero in order to determine his conception of this hero. We shall refer only to Corneille's three *Discours—Du Poème Dramatique, De la Tragédie, Des Trois Unités*—which he affixed to the 1660 edition of his dramatic work.[2]

Corneille begins by affirming that he is a disciple of Aristotle whose precepts are to be followed in the writing of dramatic poems and especially of tragedies: "Il faut suivre les précèptes de l'art. . . . Il est constant qu'il y a des précèptes puisqu'il y a un art; mais il n'est pas constant quels ils sont."[3] The last part of this sentence is interesting. Corneille agrees on the necessity of Aristotle's rules for the theatre, but he finds them obscure, and his purpose will be to interpret them: "Il faut . . . savoir quelles sont ces règles. Mais notre malheur est qu'Aristote et Horace après lui en ont écrit assez obscurément pour avoir besoin d'intérprètes."[4]

Corneille takes up Aristotle's statement that pleasure is the end of tragedy, and in the manner of many commentators before him, he draws upon Horace for the concept of the useful, "puisqu'il est impossible de plaire selon les règles, s'il ne s'y rencontre beaucoup d'utilité."[5] By introducing this new concept, Corneille is able to transform Aristotle's initial description of what the hero of a tragedy ought to be and to substitute for it in a definition not to be found in any form in Aristotle. Discussing the problem of the "naive peinture des vices et des vertus," Corneille states that it is not enough to paint virtue and vice as realistically as possible because the interest the spectator takes in the virtuous makes it necessary to end a dramatic poem by rewarding them and punishing the villains: "C'est cet intérêt qu'on aime à prendre pour les vertueux qui a obligé d'en venir à cet autre manière de finir le poème dramatique par la punition des mauvaises actions et la récompense des bonnes."[6] We recognize here the notion of poetic justice which Corneille does not label "un précèpte de l'art, mais un usage que nous avons embrassé, et dont chacun peut se départir à ses périls."[7] Consequently, it is easy for Corneille to affirm that in a tragedy, "nous avons le choix de faire un changement de bonheur en malheur ou de malheur en bonheur," a statement that contradicts Aristotle's position that the best tragedy should only develop from a happy state to an unhappy one.

Having composed arguments for a happy ending, Corneille then arrives at a definition of the hero which is also in contradiction to Aristotle's. Corneille agrees with Aristotle that a hero should be "ni tout a fait bon, ni tout à fait méchant," but he insists that the precept is valid only in theory and not in practice. He examines the examples of Oedipus and Thyestes given by Aristotle only to reject them: "J'avoue donc avec franchise que je n'entends pas l'application de cet exemple."[8] Completely misinterpreting Aristotle, Corneille cannot understand how pity and fear could result under the conditions stated: "J'avouerai plus. Si la purgation des passions se fait dans la tragédie, je tiens qu'elle se doit faire de la manière dont je l'explique; mais je doute si elle s'y fait jamais, et dans celles-la même qui ont les conditions que demande Aristote."[9]

Corneille interprets Aristotle's "catharsis" didactically:

La pitié d'un malheur où nous voyons tomber nos semblables nous porte à la crainte d'un pareil pour nous; cette crainte, au désir de l'éviter; et ce désir, à purger, modérer, rectifier, et même déraciner en nous la passion qui plonge à nos yeux dans ce malheur les personnes que nous plaignons, par cette raison commune, mais naturelle et indubitable, que pour éviter l'effet, il faut retrancher la cause.[10]

It is on these grounds that he rejects the example of Oedipus, for instance. Since Oedipus did not know his father and mother, how could he be guilty of parricide and incest? And in what manner is the audience to profit from his example? After all, not many are ready to kill their own father and commit incest with their mother. Corneille therefore believes that the purgation of pity and fear is best effected in plays written as he writes them, and he cites his own *Le Cid* as an example.

Rodrigue and Chimène are subject to passion, and it is this passion that causes their unhappiness, which in turn creates pity in the spectator:

Rodrigue et Chimène y ont cette probité sujette aux passions, et ces passions font leur malheur, puisqu'ils ne sont malheureux qu'autant qu'ils sont passionnés l'un pour l'autre. Ils tombent dans l'infélicité par cette foiblesse humaine dont nous sommes capables comme eux; leur malheur fait pitié, cela est constant, et il en a coûté assez de larmes aux spectateurs pour ne le point contester. Cette pitié nous doit donner une crainte de tomber dans un pareil malheur, et purger en nous ce trop d'amour qui cause leur infortune et nous les fait plaindre.[11]

Corneille is discerning enough to realize that the feeling of fear is indeed not very powerful in this case. He offers two explanations: one is that this fear is not spontaneous but deduced, what he calls "réfléchie"; another is that perhaps Aristotle included it only because Plato had excluded poets from his ideal republic on the ground that they created too many passions in their audiences. If Aristotle could show that these passions were purged instead of being created, then he might claim for poets the usefulness which Plato denies them: "Comme il [Aristotle] ecrivoit pour le [Plato] contredire, et montrer qu'il n'est pas à propos de les bannir des Etats bien policés, il a voulu trouver cette utilité dans ces agitations de l'âme, pour les rendre recommandables par la raison même, sur qui l'autre se fonde pour les bannir." [12] In order to avoid contradicting Aristotle, however, Corneille finds a compromise and decides that most certainly Aristotle had not meant pity and fear to be necessarily associated: the one can happen without the other, and this is especially true for fear, since ultimately pity can always produce a salutary "crainte réfléchie."

In Corneille's *Le Cid,* one experiences fear in the case of the Count (justly punished for his pride, implies Corneille,) and feels mainly pity for Rodrigue and Chimène. Corneille draws the conclusion that entirely good or bad characters should not be excluded from the theater since the former create pity and the latter fear in the spectator: J'éstime qu'il ne faut point faire de difficulté d'exposer sur la scène des hommes très vertueux ou très méchants dans le malheur." [13] After discussing the plot-subjects offered by Aristotle, Corneille finds them adequate to create pity "qui fait de si beaux effets sur nos théâtres," but offers at least one more plot which he considers better, "plus sublime"—the one in which the good are saved through the misfortune of the bad: "Sauver les bons par la perte des méchants." [14] Corneille does not presume to be a better judge than Aristotle; if Aristotle had not suggested this plot, it is because he saw no examples of it in the theater of his time: "et s'il n'en a point parlé, c'est qu'il n'en voyait point d'exemples sur les théâtres de son temps, où ce n'était pas la mode de sauver les bons par la perte des méchants." [15]

It has seemed advisable to dwell at some length on Corneille's conception of pity, fear, and poetic justice because it throws some light on the psychological portraiture of the heroic hero. Corneille, by adding the notion of the useful to that of esthetic pleasure, is able to separate the concept of pity and fear and link the first with the good characters and the second with the villains. This is very important because, by ascribing pity to heroes, he gives it a pre-eminent position which points directly to the sentimental drama of the eighteenth century. Corneille's emphasis on pity is relevant since he admires his own *Le Cid* and does not hesitate to call it a great play because it has moved its spectators to tears: "Leur malheur [Rodrigue's and Chimène's] fait pitié; cela est constant, et il en a coûté assez de larmes aux spectateurs pour ne le point contester." [16] Let us remember that *Le Cid* was first acted in 1636.

Corneille's discussion of the various components of the drama is very important in relation to Dryden's own critical writings. But, on the subject of the hero, the essential has been said: Corneille's point of view contributes much to a better understanding of the heroic drama as we have found it. The ultimate rule—that the hero should be a paragon of virtue—is not stated by Corneille in so many words, but it is to be deduced from his discussion of pity, fear, and poetic justice, and from occasional remarks related to other points, as for example:

> . . . et pour exténuer ou retrancher cette horreur dangeureuse d'une action historique, je voudrais la voir arriver sans la participation du premier acteur, pour qui nous devons toujours ménager la faveur de l'auditoire. . . . C'est un soin que nous devons prendre de préserver nos héros du crime tant qu'il se peut, et les exempter même de tremper leurs mains dans le sang si ce n'est en un juste combat. . . . Notre maxime de faire aimer nos principaux acteurs n'était pas de l'usage des anciens.[17]

In this short review of Corneille's thought, it is plain that however much he endeavored to find a *via media* with Aristotle, he not only failed, but arrived at a concept of the hero directly opposed to that of Aristotle. On the other hand, the identity between Corneille's and Dryden's thought has become clear.

An examination of one of Corneille's plays will further illustrate the similarity of the two men's dramatic work. *Horace* will be studied rather than *Le Cid* because it is probably a more typical heroic tragedy, if not as well known.

Rome and Albe are at war. [18] Horace, whose wife Sabine is from Albe, and his two brothers are chosen to fight against three Albian opponents. Horace is elated by the choice:

> Mais quoique ce combat me promette un cercueil,
> La gloire de ce choix m'enfle d'un juste orgueil;
> Mon esprit en conçoit une mâle assurance:
> J'ose espérer beaucoup de mon peu de vaillance;
> Et du sort envieux quels que soient les projets,
> Je ne me compte point pour un de vos sujets.
> Rome a trop cru de moi; mais mon âme ravie
> Remplira son attente, ou quittera la vie.
> Qui veut mourir, ou vaincre, est vaincu rarement:
> Ce noble désespoir périt malaisément.
>
> (II,i)

Curiace, his wife's brother and his friend, is not too happy at the choice, for though he wants Albe to win, he is afraid for Horace: "Ce que veut mon pays mon amitié le craint. . . . De tous les deux côtés j'ai des pleurs à répandre." Curiace, furthermore, is engaged

to Horace's sister Camille. When he learns that he and his two
brothers are Albe's choice to fight the Horaces, he accepts the responsibility but revolts at his fate:

> Que désormais le ciel, les enfers et la terre
> Unissent leurs fureurs à nous faire la guerre;
> Que les hommes, les Dieux, les démons et le sort
> Préparent contre nous un général effort!
> Je mets à faire pis, en l'état où nous sommes,
> Le sort, et les démons, et les Dieux, et les hommes,
> Ce qu'ils ont de cruel, et d'horrible et d'affreux,
> L'est bien moins que l'honneur qu'on nous fait à tous deux.

Horace, however, seems to relish his fate even more than before: to
fight for one's country is within the scope of any ordinary virtue,
but to sacrifice what one loves for the public weal, to sever all bonds
for the love of one's country is only given to heroes—those with
"âmes peu communes."

> Combattre un ennemi pour le salut de tous,
> Et contre un inconnu s'exposer seul aux coups,
> D'une simple vertu c'est l'effet ordinaire:
> Mille déjà l'ont fait, mille pourroient le faire;
> Mourir pour le pays est un si digne sort,
> Qu'on brigueroit en foule une si belle mort;
> Mais vouloir au public immoler ce qu'on aime,
> S'attacher au combat contre un autre soi-même,
> Attaquer un parti qui prend pour défenseur
> Le frère d'une femme et l'amant d'une soeur,
> Et rompant tous ces noeuds, s'armer pour la patrie
> Contre un sang qu'on voudroit racheter de sa vie,
> Une telle vertu n'appartenoit qu'à nous;
> L'éclat de son grand nom lui fait peu de jaloux,
> Et peu d'hommes au coeur l'ont assez imprimée
> Pour oser aspirer à tant de renommée.
>
> (II,iii)

Curiace acknowledges the validity of Horace's arguments, but though
he is just as ready as Horace to serve his country, he would have
preferred another means of doing so. He finds Horace's resolute attitude rather inhuman:

> Mais votre fermeté tient un peu du barbare
> . . . .
> Encor qu'à mon devoir je coure sans terreur,
> Mon coeur s'en effarouche, et j'en frémis d'horreur;
> J'ai pitié de moi-même et jette un oeil d'envie

> Sur ceux dont notre guerre a consumé la vie,
> Sans souhait toutefois de pouvoir reculer.
> Ce triste et fier honneur m'émeut sans m'ébranler:
> J'aime ce qu'il me donne, et je plains ce qu'il m'ôte;
> Et si Rome demande une vertu plus haute,
> Je rends grâces aux Dieux de n'être pas Romain,
> Pout conserver encor quelque chose d'humain.
>
> (II,iii)

But Horace is not moved:

> Contre qui que ce soit que mon pays m'emploie,
> J'accepte aveuglément cette gloire avec joie.
> . . . .
> Rome a choisi mon bras, je n'examine rien:
> Avec une allégresse aussi pleine et sincère
> Que j'épousai la soeur, je combattrai le frère;
> Et pour trancher enfin ces discours superflus,
> Albe vous a nommé, je ne vous connois plus.
>
> (II,iii)

What Horace says here is worth examining: his country calls, and he obeys blindly, "aveuglément." Far from being crushed, he feels "allégresse," and by killing Curiace, he will experience the same kind of fulfillment as he did when he married Sabine. The quality of the comparison here is indicative of his state of mind. He will abandon himself to the act of killing in the same way that he abandons himself to the act of love, and he anticipates the same type of exhilaration. The physical aspect of this comparison may not have been present in Corneille's conscious mind, but it is there, nevertheless. Horace subjects his feelings, his thoughts, his beliefs to the act he is to perform. He can only do so if he abandons himself— shuts himself away from his own consciousness—through a commitment that leads him directly to a point of no return. This shutting away is explicitly stated when he calls all this arguing "discours superflus." Words, that is ideas do not count; acts do. The submission or loss of the self is so great that in a matter of seconds Horace can assume a different identity, if identity can be defined partly as what a human being has experienced, loved, thought, up to the present time. But without one moment of hesitation, Horace is able to disown his former self in disowning Curiace: "Albe vous a nommé, je ne vous connois plus." Horace's stand is further emphasized by the character delineation of Curiace, who answers the above statement with: "Je vous connois encore, et c'est ce qui me tue."

All through the play Horace maintains the same iron determination, the same blind commitment he displays in these first scenes. When his wife begs Horace and Curiace to kill her in order to sever every link between them so that they can fight each other with no remorse, Horace is not really shaken but only puzzled. He does not face up to the problem and assume responsibility for the consequences of his act. That is, he can only view Sabine's words and acts in relation to himself and his own determination and not in relation to her own position as wife and sister:

> Que t'ai-je fait, Sabine, et quelle est mon offense
> Qui t'oblige à chercher une telle vengeance?
> Que t'a fait mon honneur, et par quel droit viens-tu
> Avec toute ta force attaquer ma vertu?
>
> (II,vi)

Indeed, what right does Sabine have to interfere? Only the right she derives from her love for him, for her brother, for her native country and her adopted one. But these motives are not even to be considered by Horace. If he is to be blind to his own fate, he has to be completely blind to his wife's.

After his brothers are killed by the Curiaces, Horace runs away from the battlefield but only in order to allow the wounded Curiaces to pursue him, thus enabling him to fight them one after the other and win the day.

When he returns, the first person he meets is his sister Camille. In this scene we have most probably Corneille's greatest stroke of genius in characterization: Horace addresses his sister before she has said anything, and his very first words are to brag of his victory. Whereas anyone else would have understood her pain, he chooses to ignore it and boasts of the very act that brings her misery.

> Ma soeur, voici le bras qui venge nos deux frères,
> Le bras qui rompt le cours de nos destins contraires,
> Qui nous rend maîtres d'Albe; enfin voici le bras
> Qui seul fait aujourd'hui le sort de deux Etats;
> Vois ces marques d'honneur, ces témoins de ma gloire,
> Et rends ce que tu dois à l'heur de ma victoire.
>
> (IV,v)

All that Camille answers is: "Recevez donc mes pleurs, c'est ce que je lui dois." But Horace will not be content with an evasive answer. He chooses to misinterpret the object of Camille's sorrow and assumes it is all for her brothers' death: "Quand la perte est vengée, on n'a plus rien perdu." Still Camille follows his lead and, with deep irony, agrees to stop crying for her brothers since they are avenged, but she adds:

> Mais qui me vengera de celle d'un amant,
> Pour me faire oublier sa perte en un moment?
> HORACE: Que dis-tu, malheureuse?
> CAMILLE: O mon cher Curiace!
>   (IV,v)

Camille's relatively subdued attitude here should be stressed, especially in view of the fact that in the preceding scene, in a long and agonizing soliloquy, she had entirely rejected her family's stand as barbarous. The scene with Horace is the famous one of Camille's "imprécations," an instance which blurs the fact of her initial meekness. All she says is "mon cher Curiace," and Horace literally leaps at her with such words as "indigne . . . insupportable audace . . . criminelle" and orders her to dominate her passion:

> O d'une indigne soeur insupportable audace!
> D'un ennemi public dont je reviens vainqueur
> Le nom est dans ta bouche et l'amour dans ton coeur!
> Ton ardeur criminelle à la vengeance aspire!
> Ta bouche la demande, et ton coeur la respire!
> Suis moins ta passion, règle mieux tes désirs,
> Ne me fais plus rougir d'entendre tes soupirs;
> Tes flammes désormais doivent être étouffées;
> Bannis-les de ton âme, et songe à mes trophées:
> Qu'ils soient dorénavant ton unique entretien.
>   (IV,v)

It is only after this that Camille bursts out with her "imprécations," beginning: "Donne-moi donc, barbare, un coeur comme le tien," and ending: "Voir le dernier Romain à son dernier soupir, / Moi seule en être cause, et mourir de plaisir!" Camille is not the one who provokes Horace's wrath. It is rather he who provokes her into the passionate assertion of her fidelity to Curiace's memory. This is very important, for Horace accuses Camille of treason before she has proclaimed herself against Rome—solely on the grounds of her sorrow as lover. He wants her to be not only true to Rome, but also happy about the outcome. One feels that when Horace kills Camille, he is not trying to suppress the traitor so much as the sufferer—that is, the one who stands for the relative as against the absolute value of things. Horace's world has no room for the likes of Camille; she must be suppressed, and Horace kills her. Ironically, he has just told her to dominate her passions: "Suis moins ta passion, règle mieux tes désirs." As to Horace himself, he dominates his passions indeed, when the passions are love for his wife, friendship, pity for a sister's misfortunes. But anger at a sister's sorrow is a passion he cannot dominate, and it carries him to the point of committing murder.

It would be wrong to assume that pity and understanding are foreign to Corneille's heroic world; all through the play Sabine and Curiace exemplify such feelings without any shade of dishonor being cast upon them. Indeed, Curiace is not one iota less honorable than Horace at any moment in the play. Furthermore, in Corneille's own time, Camille's murder by Horace was considered a blemish in the play. D'Aubignac, for instance, in his *Pratique du Théâtre,* says:

La mort de Camille par la main d'Horace, son frère, n'a pas été approuvée au théâtre, bien que ce soit une aventure véritable, et j'avois été d'avis, pour sauver en quelque sorte l'histoire, et tout ensemble la bienséance de la scène que cette fille désespérée, voyant son frère l'épée à la main, se fut précipitée dessus: ainsi elle fut morte de la main d'Horace, et lui eut été digne de compassion comme un malheureux innocent; l'histoire et le théâtre auroient été d'accord.[19]

In the *Examen* affixed to his play Corneille acknowledges this blemish most candidly and even adds arguments against it: "Tous veulent que la mort de Camille en gâte la fin, et j'en demeure d'accord; mais je ne sais si tous en savent la raison." [20] He points out that this action has not been prepared for in the plot and is not really linked to the main action:

Elle surprend tout d'un coup; et toute la préparation que j'y ai donnée par la peinture de la vertu farouche d'Horace, et par la défense qu'il fait à sa soeur de regretter qui que ce soit, de lui ou de son amant, qui meure au combat, n'est point suffisante pour faire attendre un emportement si extraordinaire, et servir de commencement à cette action.[21]

It is exciting to see an author carried away, so to speak, by his own characterization; Corneille seems to be as surprised as any spectator at the violence of Horace's reaction. Furthermore, he stresses the gratuity of Horace's act:

Horace revient triomphant, sans aucun besoin de tuer sa soeur, ni même de parler à elle; et l'action seroit suffisamment terminée à sa victoire. Cette chute d'un péril en l'autre, sans nécessité, fait ici un effet d'autant plus mauvais, que d'un péril public, où il y va de tout l'Etat, il tombe en un péril particulier, où il n'y va que de sa vie, et pour dire encore plus, d'un péril illustre, où il ne peut succomber que glorieusement, en un péril infâme, dont il ne peut sortir sans tache.[22]

But Corneille does not even attempt to explain away these faults of the play. The closest he comes to a refutation is that Camille's murder by Horace is a historical fact. When one considers the liberties which Corneille habitually took with history, one can indeed doubt the validity of this excuse.

From our point of view, however, this murder is the stroke of genius which, in *Horace*, brings the characterization to the heroic hero to such a point of perfection that he transcends himself and attains his contrary—that is, he becomes an antihero: the hero can face anything except his own self. For if Horace were to understand Camille and to agree that the reason for her sorrow could be valid, he would be acknowledging the existence of values he has once and for all rejected. It would mean entering a world of feelings and passions which he does not want to enter. To accept Camille's sorrow would give it a reality which would challenge the validity of his own act. It would mean a break in the solidity of the wall with which he has surrounded himself. An attempt to understand Camille might lead him to want to understand himself, and this would be the negation of Horace's very existence. Once and for all, he has adopted a scale of values which for him has taken the place of motives. His complete subjection to that scale of values enables him to think by acts, so to speak: the act is entitled to a value judgment but not the motive.

However, this can be the case only if one assumes that this scale of values is absolute and unchallenged. Camille questions it, so Horace has to kill her. By killing her, he kills that part of himself which he wants subjected; he kills that other self which could have existed. He seems to be speaking as much of himself as of Camille when he says, "et ce souhait impie, encore qu'impuissant, / Est un monstre qu'il faut étouffer en naissant" (IV,vi).

It is the murder of Camille which, far from taking all human feeling away from Horace, actually restores him to his place among other human beings. Through this murder he becomes nothing more than a man afraid to look into himself. This negation of self, this complete surrender to a code of conduct evolved for him by others, is what makes of Horace a character with an extremely modern psychology, a type of character which has rarely been found so profusely until our century, for rarely has indoctrination attained such perfection in the past.

Turning to Racine, one enters a world altogether different. It would be tempting to choose *Phèdre* since it is probably not only Racine's most typical play, but also the one in which he attains the summit of his art as dramatist. However, for purposes of studying the heroic play, it may be best to turn to *Bérénice*, for in many aspects it is a heroic play; and yet it is very different from any of Corneille's or Dryden's dramas. Actually it is precisely when *Bérénice* comes closest to being a heroic play that the differences between the two schools of drama become more evident.

To delineate a Racinean plot is no easy task, for one is faced with two alternatives: to give the plot or fable in one or two sentences, or to enter minutely into a close analysis of the action. With a play by Corneille or Dryden the problem is one of simplification: the events which constitute the action are so numerous that one is at a loss to decide which to take up and which to leave. But with Racine the plot is so simple that no such problem exists, and *Bérénice* is probably the play with the simplest plot of all. Racine himself, translating from Suetonius, gives it in one sentence: "Titus, qui aimoit passionement Bérénice, et qui même, à ce qu'on croyoit, lui avoit promis de l'épouser, la renvoya de Rome, malgré lui et malgré elle, dès les premiers jours de son empire." [23] We recognize here the heroic theme of love versus duty which so many misguided critics thought they found in Dryden's heroic plays. Titus, though passionately in love with Bérénice, obeys the call of duty and forsakes her. According to Racine it is the very simplicity of the plot that appealed to him: "Mais ce qui m'en plut davantage, c'est que je le trouvai extrêmement simple. Il y avoit longtemps que je voulois essayer si je pourrois faire une tragédie avec cette simplicité d'action qui a été si fort du goût des anciens." [24]

In view of this simplicity of plot, to study the play will be more a matter of analyzing it than of summarizing it, that is, a matter of examining how things happen rather than what happens.

During the first act, Antiochus, an Oriental king and a friend of both Titus and Bérénice, learns of her rumored nuptials with Titus and reveals his love for her and his plans for an imminent departure.[25] Bérénice, in this first scene of hers, radiates both happiness and self-assurance in her answer to Antiochus:

Seigneur, je n'ai pas cru que dans une journée
Qui doit avec César unir ma destinée,
Il fût quelque mortel qui pût impunément
Se venir à mes yeux déclarer mon amant.
Mais de mon amitié mon silence est un gage:
J'oublie en sa faveur un discours qui m'outrage.
Je n'en ai point troublé le cours injurieux.
Je fais plus: à regret je reçois vos adieux.
Le ciel sait qu'au milieu des honneurs qu'il m'envoie,
Je n'attendois que vous pour témoin de ma joie.
Avec tout l'univers j'honorois vos vertus;
Titus vous chérissoit, vous admiriez Titus.
Cent fois je me suis fait une douceur extrême
D'entretenir Titus dans un autre lui-même.

(I,iv)

Bérénice is sure that finally Titus is going to marry her: "dans une journée / Qui doit avec César unir ma destinée"; her use of the name Caesar instead of Titus is indicative of her mood. Though pained at the loss of a friend, she is apparently really thinking of herself instead of Antiochus; otherwise her unconscious cruelty, in giving him the reasons why she would have wanted him to stay, would be incomprehensible: "Cent fois je me suis fait une douceur extrême / D'entretenir Titus dans un autre lui-même." Only a woman engrossed in her own happy state would be so impervious to another's suffering. Antiochus is not duped: "Et c'est ce que je fuis. J'évite, mais trop tard, /Ces cruels entretiens où je n'ai point de part" (I,iv).

When Antiochus leaves Bérénice, her confidant is full of pity for him and asks, "Ne le plaignez-vous pas?" Bérénice should have answered, "Yes, I pity him." Instead, she again refuses to consider Antiochus' condition in relation to her own suffering, and displays the same egoistical concern she had shown him in the previous scene. "Cette prompte retraite / Me laisse, je l'avoue, une douleur secrète." When Phénice suggests that Bérénice should have kept Antiochus as an alternative in case Titus proves fickle, Bérénice spurns the suggestion: "Le temps n'est plus, Phénice, où je pouvois trembler. / Titus m'aime; il peut tout." In other words, since Titus loves her, Bérénice feels all-powerful. She has the careless self-assurance usually associated with those whom life has spared as yet. She is thrilled by all the pomp and splendor in which she is going to participate, to the point of exhilaration:

De cette nuit, Phénice, as-tu vu la splendeur?
Tes yeux ne sont-ils pas tous pleins de sa grandeur?
Ces flambeaux, ce bûcher, cette nuit enflammée,
Ces aigles, ces faisceaux, ce peuple, cette armée,
Cette foule de rois, ces consuls, ce sénat,
Qui tous de mon amant empruntoient leur éclat;
Cette pourpre, cet or, qui rehaussoit sa gloire,
Et ces lauriers encor témoins de sa victoire.

(I,v)

The first act ends on a triumphal note from Bérénice:

Que tardons-nous? Allons, pour son empire heureux,
Au ciel, qui le protège, offrir aussi nos voeux.
Aussitôt, sans l'attendre et sans être attendue,
Je reviens le chercher, et dans cette entrevue
Dire tout ce qu'aux coeurs l'un de l'autre contents
Inspirent des transports retenus si longtemps.

(I,v)

The first words of Titus in the second act are to ask for Antiochus. Until then, the audience knows Titus only through descriptions by both Antiochus and Bérénice. The overall portrait derived from these descriptions is the one usually reserved for heroes in heroic plays. Even Antiochus has to acknowledge the virtue of his rival: "La valeur de Titus surpassoit ma fureur. / Il faut qu'à sa vertu mon estime réponde" (I,iv).

We saw Bérénice leave the stage in an exalted mood. When Titus enters, he is far from answering the triumphal description Bérénice has just given of him. His attitude is rather business-like and sad. When informed of Bérénice's gratitude, he answers with: "Trop aimable princesse! Hélas!" Titus wants his adviser Paulin to inform him faithfully and exactly of Rome's feelings about his marriage with Bérénice. We recognize here, of course, a reversal in the action: Bérénice's happiness if far from being as assured as she thinks; it is still in question, and ironically, the one whom she relies on for her happiness, Titus, is the very one who is endangering it. Paulin voices Rome's adverse feelings but assures Titus that it will follow him, even though not wholeheartedly. But Titus has already made up his mind: he wanted to know the opinion of Rome only to reinforce him in his decision:

Malgré tout mon amour, Paulin, et tous ses charmes,
Après mille serments appuyés de mes larmes,

Maintenant que je puis couronner tant d'attraits,
Maintenant que je l'aime encor plus que jamais,
Lorsqu'un heureux hymen, joignant nos destinées,
Peut payer en un jour les voeux de cinq années,
Je vais, Paulin. . . . O ciel! puis-je le déclarer?
PAULIN: Quoi, Seigneur?
TITUS: Pour jamais je vais m'en séparer.
Mon coeur en ce moment ne vient pas de se rendre.
Si je t'ai fait parler, si j'ai voulu t'entendre,
Je voulois que ton zèle achevât en secret
De confondre un amour qui se tait à regret.
Bérénice a longtemps balancé la victoire;
Et si je penche enfin du côté de ma gloire,
Crois qu'il m'en a couté, pour vaincre tant d'amour,
Des combats dont mon coeur saignera plus d'un jour.
                                              (II,ii)

Actually, Titus's only problem is to find a way in which to break
the news to Bérénice. But he feels he has delayed too long; she
must leave as soon as possible, and he wants Antiochus to take
her back. This reinforces the fact of his having arrived at a decision before he comes on stage since his very first words are to in-
quire about Antiochus' whereabouts. We know now that it is to
escort Bérénice back to her kingdom.

J'attends Antiochus pour lui recommander
Ce dépôt precieux que je ne puis garder.
Jusque dans l'Orient je veux qu'il la ramène.
Demain Rome avec lui verra partir la Reine.
Elle en sera bientôt instruite par ma voix,
Et je vais lui parler pour la dernière fois.
                                      (II,ii)

The situation offered the audience is then a tragic one: at the time
when Bérénice thinks her fortunes are at their highest, they have
never been in fact at a lower ebb.

Paulin can only commend Titus: "Et qu'un héros vainqueur de
tant de nations / Sauroit bien, tôt ou tard, vaincre ses passions"
(II,ii). But Titus is far from feeling the exhilaration and self-
assurance of the usual heroic hero! His eyes are open to his own
cruelty: "Ah! que sous de beaux noms cette gloire est cruelle." His
love for Bérénice had made a better man of him: "Je lui dois tout,
Paulin." But how does he reward her? "Récompense cruelle."
Horace's actions and attitude, as we have seen, were termed cruel
and barbarous; the one important difference is that these terms

were used by others to qualify Horace, whereas Titus applies
these terms to his own behavior. Far from making Bérénice responsible for his difficult choice and accusing her of drawing him away
from duty—as Horace accuses Sabine—Titus is all sympathy and
identifies himself completely with Bérénice's situation:

> Récompense cruelle!
> Tout ce que je lui dois va retomber sur elle.
> Pour prix de tant de gloire et de tant de vertus,
> Je lui dirai: "Partez, et ne me voyez plus."
>
> (II,ii)

This capacity for sympathy gives the measure of Titus's love:

> Je connois Bérénice, et ne sais que trop bien
> Que son coeur n'a jamais demandé que le mien.
> Je l'aimai, je lui plus. Depuis cette journée
> (Dois-je dire funeste, hélas! ou fortunée?)
> Sans avoir en aimant d'objet que son amour,
> Etrangère dans Rome, inconnue à la cour,
> Elle passe ses jours, Paulin, sans rien prétendre
> Que quelque heure à me voir, et le reste à m'attendre.
> Encor si quelquefois un peu moins assidu
> Je passe le moment où je suis attendu,
> Je la revois bientôt de pleurs toute trempée.
> Ma main à les sécher est longtemps occupée.
> Enfin tout ce qu'Amour a de noeuds plus puissants,
> Doux reproches, transports sans cesse renaissants,
> Soin de plaire sans art, crainte toujours nouvelle,
> Beauté, gloire, vertu, je trouve tout en elle.
> Depuis cinq ans entiers chaque jour je la vois,
> Et crois toujours la voir pour la première fois.
>
> (II,ii)

The wound he is ready to inflict upon Bérénice probably hurts him
more than it will hurt her. When finally the two meet, he finds
himself unable to inform her of his decision and leaves her hastily,
half choking on the words, "Rome . . . l'Empire. . . ."

Bérénice in this last scene of the second act, is left much less sure
of her position than at the end of the first act:

> Quoi? me quitter sitôt, et ne me dire rien?
> Chère Phénice, hélas! quel funeste entretien!
> Qu'ai-je fait? Que veut-il? Et que dit ce silence?
>
> (II,v)

She considers the possibility that Titus might take the side of
Rome, but rejects it:

> Il craint peut-être, il craint d'épouser une reine.
> Hélas! s'il étoit vrai . . . . Mais non, il a cent fois
> Rassuré mon amour contre leurs dures lois. . . .
> (II,v)

She prefers to think that, informed of Antiochus' love for her, Titus is jealous: "L'amour d'Antiochus l'a peut-être offensé." In this case, she has nothing to fear:

> Allons, Phénice, un mot pourra le satisfaire.
> Rassurons-nous, mon coeur, je puis encor lui plaire:
> Je me comptois trop tôt au rang des malheureux.
> Si Titus est jaloux, Titus est amoureux.
> (II,v)

At this point, Bérénice is not as triumphant, but she is still deluded as to her fortunes.

Titus meanwhile informs Antiochus of his resolution:

> Telle est ma destinée
> Pour elle et pour Titus il n'est plus d'hyménée.
> D'un espoir si charmant je me flattois en vain:
> Prince, il faut avec vous qu'elle parte demain.
> (III,i)

Far from taking pride in it, he asks Antiochus to pity him:

> Plaignez ma grandeur importune.
> Maître de l'univers, je règle sa fortune;
> Je puis faire les rois, je puis les déposer:
> Cependant de mon coeur je ne puis disposer.
> (III,i)

Since Antiochus is such a good friend, Titus asks him to break the news to Bérénice and begs of him to take good care of her:

> Adieu; ne quittez point ma princesse, ma reine,
> Tout ce qui de mon coeur fut l'unique désir,
> Tout ce que j'aimerai jusqu'au dernier soupir.
> (III,i)

Antiochus is at a loss: should he rejoice or not? He knows Bérénice too well to hope for much. Yet, his situation can hardly become worse. Any change is for the better. But face to face with Bérénice, he does not feel strong enough to tell her the news. It is only her repeated pleadings that finally force him to do it:

ANTIOCHUS: Titus m'a commandé . . . .
BÉRÉNICE: Quoi?
ANTIOCHUS: De vous déclarer

Qu'a jamais l'un de l'autre il faut vous séparer.
BÉRÉNICE; Nous séparer? Qui? Moi? Titus de Bérénice!

(III,iii)

Bérénice cannot believe the news. Titus loves her too much. His honor forbids him to leave her: "Il ne me quitte point, il y va de sa gloire. . . . Titus m'aime. Titus ne veut point que je meure." All that Antiochus tells her is a scheme designed by him to try to part her from Titus. Her cruelty towards Antiochus has never reached a higher point since, when she accuses him of treason, she feels her argument is only a way to deceive herself: "Hélas! pour me tromper je fais ce que je puis" (III,iii).

Antiochus is crushed by the irony of his situation:

Je me verrai puni parce qu'il est coupable?
Avec quelle injustice et quelle indignité
Elle doute à mes yeux de ma sincerité!
Titus l'aime, dit-elle, et moi je l'ai trahie.
L'ingrate! m'accuser de cette perfidie!
Et dans quel temps encor? Dans le moment fatal
Que j'étale à ses yeux les pleurs de mon rival;
Que, pour la consoler, je le faisois paraître
Amoureux et constant, plus qu'il ne l'est peut-être.

(III,iv)

Antiochus has made up his mind never to see Bérénice any more. Yet the third act ends with his sending his confidant after Bérénice to make sure she does not attempt anything violent that would endanger her life: "Va voir si la douleur ne l'a point saisie. / Cours; et partons du moins assurés de sa vie (III,iv).

The play has reached its climax. Bérénice is in possession of the facts. The problem is stated: Titus is determined she should go, and she knows it. The question is: what will she do? Or rather, what will she feel? When and how is she going to reach the stage of recognition?

At her own request, Titus is about to face Bérénice; understandably, he is frightened. Now that she knows, she will try to influence him. He is not sure of the outcome of the battle between both their wills, especially since he is quite cognizant of what he owes her and recognizes the cruel and barbarous quality of his duty. In a passionate soliloquy he goes over the problem once more:

Hé bien! Titus, que viens-tu faire?
Bérénice t'attend. Ou viens-tu, téméraire?

> Tes adieux sont-ils prêts? T'es-tu bien consulté?
> Ton coeur te promet-il assez de cruauté?
> Car enfin au combat qui pour toi se prépare
> C'est peu d'être constant, il faut être barbare.
> Soutiendrai-je ces yeux dont la douce langueur
> Sait si bien découvrir les chemins de mon coeur?
> Quand je verrai ces yeux armés de tous les charmes,
> Attachés sur les miens, m'accabler de leurs larmes,
> Me souviendrai-je alors de mon triste devoir?
>
> (IV,iv)

Self-righteousness is certainly not one of Titus's failings. How can it be? It is possible for Corneille's heroes to be self-righteous; all that is asked of them is that they know what they are supposed to do and do it. They are not responsible for the laws they follow. Titus's case is different. He is in a position to make his own laws. This is clearly stated all through the play. Titus is not blinded by his sense of duty; he can see its drawbacks, and he accepts the responsibility for the consequences of following it. He does what he does not out of blind commitment, but through a search for motives which leaves him aware of the nature of his actions, and allows him to qualify them with such words as "cruauté . . . barbare . . . triste devoir." He is lucid where Corneille's heroes are blind. Given the same act—the one judges it; the other obeys the order to do it.

When Titus finally meets Bérénice and she strikes out at him with: "Hé bien, il est donc vrai que Titus m'abandonne? / Il faut nous séparer et c'est lui qui l'ordonne," he tries to help her transcend her own situation. Bérénice has reached her lowest point; cast away, wild with anguish, she is ready to fight with whatever weapons she can avail herself of while Titus endeavors to appeal to her better nature:

> Rappelez bien plutôt ce coeur, qui tant de fois
> M'a fait de mon devoir reconnoitre la voix.
> Il en est temps. Forcez votre amour à se taire;
> Et d'un oeil que la gloire et la raison éclaire
> Contemplez mon devoir dans toute sa rigueur.
> Vous-même contre vous fortifiez mon coeur.
>
> (IV,v)

He is actually asking Bérénice to become what the heroine in Dryden's heroic plays generally is. The most important factor, however, is that here it is he, the hero, who is showing the heroine the way to duty, whereas in Dryden's plays it is she who performs this role.

Bérénice, however, cannot forgive him so easily, for she holds him responsible, and rightly so. Horace was chosen to perform his duty and Sabine could blame fate for her misfortunes. But no compulsion, except an inner sense of duty, forces Titus to renounce his love, and Bérénice is cognizant of this fact:

> Quand votre heureux amour peut tout ce qu'il désire,
> Lorsque Rome se tait, quand votre père expire,
> Lorsque tout l'univers fléchit à vos genoux,
> Enfin quand je n'ai plus à redouter que vous.

To which Titus makes the assertion of his individual will:

> Et c'est moi seul aussi qui pouvois me détruire.
> Je pouvois vivre alors et me laisser séduire.
> Mon coeur se gardoit bien d'aller dans l'avenir
> Chercher ce qui pouvoit un jour nous désunir.
> Je voulois qu'a mes voeux rien ne fût invincible;
> Je n'examinois rien, j'espérois l'impossible.
> Que sais-je? j'espérois de mourir à vos yeux,
> Avant que d'en venir à ces cruels adieux.
> Les obstacles sembloient renouveler ma flamme.
> Tout l'Empire parloit; mais la gloire, Madame,
> Ne s'étoit point encor fait entendre à mon coeur
> Du ton dont elle parle au coeur d'un empereur.
>
> (IV,v)

This statement throws light on the different quality of the Racinean concept of honor as opposed to the Cornelian. In Corneille's tragedies, as in Dryden's, duty has an absolute value unrelated to the circumstances which create it. That is, whatever the circumstances, a hero can act in only one way. Horace has to fight the Curiaces; the fact that they are his friends and brothers-in-law has no bearing on the quality of his duty. But for Titus the problem presents itself in an entirely different way: when his country, his father, the Senate opposed his love for Bérénice, he defied them. But when all outside interference is removed, when he is left face to face with his own self, it is then that his duty to his country takes on its full value. What is permissible for Titus the citizen becomes out of range of Titus the emperor, the personification of all power. Where Horace finds fulfillment and physical exhilaration, Titus finds a sort of spiritual death: "Mais il ne s'agit plus de

vivre, il faut régner." He is not even afraid to carry the assumption
to actual physical death:

> J'espère que bientôt la triste renommée
> Vous fera confesser que vous étiez aimée.
> Vous verrez que Titus n'a pu sans éxpirer . . . .
>
> (IV,iv)

When Bérénice offers to stay with him even though he does not
marry her, he seems to relent: "Demeurez." But he overwhelms
Bérénice with examples of heroic behavior taken from Roman history; even Bérénice has to understand his reluctance. Proudly she
leaves him, with the weight of her intended suicide on his conscience.

Titus wants to rush after her, but Paulin stops him: Bérénice is
being watched; she is in no danger. Besides, Titus should not feel
crushed:

> Mais regardez plus loin: songez en ce malheur,
> Quelle gloire va suivre un moment de douleur,
> Quels applaudissements l'univers vous prépare,
> Quel rang dans l'avenir.
>
> (IV,vi)

This is the image of the heroic hero as he sees himself in Corneille's
and Dryden's plays, but this is not how Titus sees himself: "Non, je
suis un barbare. Moi-même je me hais." Horace is proud of his
fate. Titus deplores it: "Ah, Rome! Ah, Bérénice! Ah, prince malheureux! / Pourquoi suis-je empereur? Pourquoi suis-je amoureux?"

Antiochus rushes in to beg him to go to Bérénice: "Bérénice va
peut-être expirer dans les bras de Phénice." He must go to her or
renounce all claim to humanity: "Sauvez tant de vertus, de grâces,
de beauté, / Ou renoncez, Seigneur, à toute humanité" (IV,vii).
But Paulin, on the other hand, informs him that the Senate is wait-
ing for him. Titus goes to the Senate, once more asking Antiochus
to replace him at Bérénice's side. However, his last words are am-
biguous: "Voyez la Reine. Allez. J'espère à mon retour / Qu'elle ne
pourra plus douter de mon amour" (IV,viii).

At the start of Act V, the problem is still unresolved. Bérénice has
reached utter despair and is ready to die. Titus is torn by his
love for her and comes back from the Senate ready to show her
how much he loves her. Antiochus assumes that this proof of his
love can only mean that Titus has at last relented and told the

Senate he has decided to marry Bérénice. When Titus goes to her, Bérénice is all sarcasm:

> Retournez, retournez vers ce sénat auguste
> Qui vient vous applaudir de votre cruauté.
> Hé bien! avec plaisir l'avez-vous écouté?
> Etes-vous pleinement content de votre gloire?
> Avez-vous bien promis d'oublier ma mémoire?
> Mais ce n'est pas assez expier vos amours:
> Avez-vous bien promis de me haïr toujours?
>
> (V,v)

When Titus assures her that he has told the Senate nothing and that he loves her, she replies: "Vous m'aimez, vous me le soutenez; / Et cependant je pars, et vous me l'ordonnez!" In her hand is a letter which Titus seizes and reads: it was meant to be read by him after her death, for her departure was only a stratagem to enable her to commit suicide more freely. Titus sends for Antiochus and turns to Bérénice. His tone is stern and business-like and is the more powerful for it. He tells her that his sufferings are even greater than he expected them to be. He is ashamed of his own behavior since he can think of nothing but his love and concern for her. He has not even told Rome of his decision to part from her. When he comes to her, what does he find? Imminent death. This is too much: "C'en est trop. Ma douleur, à cette triste vue, / A son dernier excès est enfin parvenue." He has reached the limit of his suffering. But this does not mean he has changed his mind. He never will:

> Ne vous attendez point que las de tant d'alarmes,
> Par un heureux hymen je tarisse vos larmes.
> En quelque extrémité que vous m'ayez réduit,
> Ma gloire inexorable à toute heure me suit:
> Sans cesse elle présente à mon âme étonnée
> L'Empire incompatible avec votre hyménée,
> Me dit qu'après l'éclat et les pas que j'ai faits,
> Je dois vous épouser encor moins que jamais.
>
> (V,vi)

Titus is a Roman. When Romans are cornered, they know one noble way out. Consequently, if Bérénice should persist in her design, she will have his blood on her hands:

> Si vos pleurs plus longtemps viennent frapper ma vue,
> Si toujours à mourir je vous vois résolue,
> S'il faut qu'à tous moments je tremble pour vos jours,

> Si vous ne me jurez d'en respecter le cours,
> Madame, à d'autres pleurs vous devez vous attendre:
> En l'état où je suis, je puis tout entreprendre,
> Et je ne reponds pas que ma main à vos yeux
> N'ensanglante à la fin nos funestes adieux.
>
> (V,vi)

Antiochus comes in thinking Titus and Bérénice are reconciled and ready to be married. He tells Titus of his love for Bérénice, which he has been unable to surmount: "Pour ne la plus aimer j'ai cent fois combattu: / Je n'ai pu l'oublier." The only solution for him is death.

Bérénice, who all this time has been seated, stands up:

> Arrêtez, arrêtez. Princes trop généreux,
> En quelle extrémité me jetez-vous tous deux!
> Soit que je vous regarde, ou que je l'envisage,
> Partout du désespoir je rencontre l'image.
> Je ne vois que des pleurs, et je n'entends parler
> Que de trouble, d'horreurs, de sang prêt à couler.
>
> (V,vii)

She turns to Titus. Finally, she is convinced he loves her. That is all she wanted. She will prove to him she loves him just as much— she will go on living:

> Je crois, depuis cinq ans jusqu'à ce dernier jour,
> Vous avoir assuré d'un véritable amour.
> Ce n'est pas tout: je veux, en ce moment funeste,
> Par un dernier effort couronner tout le reste.
> Je vivrai, je suivrai vos ordres absolus.
> Adieu, Seigneur, régnez: je ne vous verrai plus.
>
> (V,vii)

Turning to Antiochus, she asks him to follow her example:

> Sur Titus et sur moi réglez votre conduite.
> Je l'aime, je le fuis: Titus m'aime, il me quitte.
> Portez loin de mes yeux vos soupirs et vos fers.
>
> (V,vii)

Her last words are for Titus: "Pour la dernière fois, adieu, Seigneur."

Titus is a heroic hero. Not once does he falter in his determination to perform what he considers his duty; and what he does is for "la gloire." There is no doubt that "gloire" for Titus means inner self-respect. He repeatedly rejects the popular praise which Paulin keeps mentioning in order to bolster his spirits. He cannot be bothered with it. His problem is inner. How can he face himself if as emperor he fails his own people, those who have put their trust in him? It is the essential different quality in the scale of values to which they refer that separates the Cornelian and Drydenian from the Racinian hero. Titus creates his own duty; it originates in him, and he is ready to bear the responsibilities it entails, even when these responsibilities mean the loss of all that he considers worth living for. This is why *Bérénice* has to end tragically. Titus must be made conscious of the adverse consequences of his decision to give it its full value. Since he is responsible for his act, if this act means the eventual acquirement of further happiness, in what manner would this act be heroic?

For the Cornelian and Drydenian hero, the logic of their case demands a happy ending. They did not take the responsibility for their act; society (or authority) did. And society (or authority) has to reward them if it wants other heroes to follow their example. The concept of eventual reward is essential to all doctrinaire or dogmatic philosophies, governments, or religions. They demand complete trust of the individual, complete denial of the self, in return for the promised land—if not in this world, then in the next, if not in this generation, then in the next. "Denial of the self" is purposely used here in contrast to what can be termed "self-denial" in Titus. The Cornelian hero denies himself all self-expression to the extent that he becomes the personification of the better qualities which society wants to find in its members. This hero is a superman because he is the common denominator of the best individuals which make up a group. In no way does he transcend himself, since at no time does he give expression to that self, unless a low physical attraction to a member of the opposite sex can be termed "expression of the self." The Racinean hero on the contrary, attains true self-denial. Titus knows he can expect no reward; he knows that only death, both emotional and physical, awaits him; yet, he performs his duty. He can do nothing else since this duty is a reflection of his very inner being; it is a part of himself; he has worked it out and has assumed its responsibilities; in short, it is through expression of his inner self that he can attain self-denial. We recognize here, of course, an important aspect of the Jansenist tenets, which puzzle many when they are first acquainted with the ideology of the movement. If grace is predestined and nothing of what we do, or do not, on this earth matters, then why should we act rightly? Titus gives a partial answer: it is to satisfy neither man nor God but the inner self. This does not in any way imply self-satisfaction. Self-satisfaction is a kind of reward, and it is rejected precisely on those grounds; Titus condemns himself with such words as "barbare" and "cruel." It is only that sense of duty is part of man's character and is to be given expression. This is the reason why Titus nevers wavers in his decision. He has looked into himself, examined his motives, and arrived at the conclusion as to what is right and wrong. This self-reliance, this self-analysis is, of course, what brings Jansenism so close to Protestant movements, and what made it at all times a heresy in the eyes of the Catholic church.

Unlike Titus, many of the heroes we have examined in Dryden's plays, at one moment or another, waver in the performance of their duty. This is quite understandable since their duty does not originate within themselves but must always be present in front of their eyes; when blinded by one thing or another (usually their physical desire for the woman they love), they lose sight of their duty and need a helping hand to keep them going. This helping hand, as we have seen, is more often than not, the heroine's. In Corneille's *Titus et Bérénice*, Bérénice performs that role for Titus. In their last scene together, when he inquires, "L'amour peut-il se faire une si douce loi?" Bérénice answers: "La raison me la fait malgré vous, malgré moi." Corneille's Bérénice stands for reason. Racine's stands for love. Not once in her last scene does she use the word reason. It is her love that made her better, not her reason:

> Adieu; servons tous trois d'exemple à l'univers
> De l'amour la plus tendre et la plus malheureuse
> Dont il puisse garder l'histoire douloureuse.
>
> (V,vii)

This shows that Racine's Bérénice is the heroine of the play, because it is she who undergoes development and eventually transcends the limitations of her egotistical self through love and renunciation. And Titus helps her do this.

If we now consider the technique which Corneille and Racine used in their respective drama, we shall find that it varies immensely from one author to the other. Georges May has a valuable study on the subject in which he examines the plays in terms of

their dramatic value—"du point de vue de l'intérêt qu'elles suscit-
ent." [26] He finds them to be diametrically opposed because the purposes of the playwrights are opposed. According to May, Corneille
displays excellent showmanship because he is interested in the
intrigue or action. Racine despises intrigue or action because he is
interested in human passions:

Pour susciter et maintenir l'intérêt, Corneille n'hésite pas à utiliser au
maximum ce qu'il y a précisément de plus materiel dans la matière
tragique. Racine, au contraire, n'a pour l'intrigue qu'un mépris absolu.
Il ne l'accepte que parce qu'il lui est impossible de faire autrement,
parce que sans intrigue, les passions n'ont plus aucune raison, plus
aucun prétexte pour se manifester, et parce que c'est justement vers
l'analyse et l'étude de ces passions déchaînées que va sa prédilection
d'écrivain.[27]

May seems to oppose intrigue and passions as if they belonged
to a common domain, for he contends that one is the forte of
Corneille and the other of Racine. More specifically, he says that
Racine spurns intrigue because he is interested in the passions,
whereas Corneille relies heavily on it. But he does not say why.
At another point in the study, however, he gives what seems to be
a partial answer. He states that Corneille wanted above all else
to please his audience and that he knew the best way to achieve
this was to work on the emotions of the public: "C'est avec, en
tête, cet objectif essentiel de plaire et donc d'émouvoir que Corneille
aborde le théâtre, et c'est vers ce but que nous le voyons aller con-
stamment de toute la force pas toujours heureuse de son instinct
dramatique." [28] The emotional response which Corneille expects
from his audience is not one of pity or fear but rather one of
admiration, through what May terms "le Nietzscheisme avant la
lettre." That is, he accepts the traditional concept of Corneille's
hero as admirable, a superman, an idealized personification of
what each individual ought to be: "un surhomme qui rappelle
l'idéal des hommes de la Renaissance, et préfigure en même temps
l'homme surhumain de Nietzsche." [29]

Having identified the nature of the Cornelian heroic hero, I
believe the reason Corneille relies on intrigue and what May calls
the "outrance" of a situation and characterization is that his art is
rhetorical. The purpose of his drama is to carry the spectator
away and win him over before he has had time to reflect. Racine's
purpose is, on the contrary, to open the eyes of the spectator, that

is, make him look into the deepest darkest recesses of a character
and of himself. This is one reason why I find it so difficult to agree
entirely with May and those critics who hold the view that Corneille paints men as they should be and Racine, as they are. Corneille's art is escapist, and we are all more or less escapists. But
where is the person who analyzes his own inner motives and impulses, and especially who condemns himself in the manner that
Racine's characters do? On the other hand, the rhetorical power
of Corneille's plays has often been put to the test. For instance,
Corneille's *Horace* was the play most often acted by the Comédie
Française during World War I.

Whatever the ends which he ascribes to Corneille's and Racine's
theatre, Georges May's analysis of their respective techniques is
essentially valid. From the standpoint of the study of Dryden's
plays, this analysis is interesting, for more often than not, what
is valid for Corneille is equally valid for Dryden.

Dryden's plays, like Corneille's, are mainly intrigue, an accumulation of events which carry the spectator from climax to climax,
through suspense and surprise. Like Corneille, Dryden is fond of
revealing his hero in situations demanding the utmost valor. It is
this purpose, according to May, which draws Corneille towards
the "invraisemblable." History provides him with "le point de
départ et l'aboutissement de son action." In between, he feels free
to fill the gap as he pleases. We can also recognize Dryden in this
description. Dryden used historical facts and characters—the conquest of Mexico by the Spaniards, the fall of Granada, Maximin
and Saint Catherine—but he was not faithful to them. To provoke
the imagination, he needed free rein and could not allow himself
to be limited by history. As drama, his plays, like Corneille's were
of his own invention. Even in such works as *Oedipus, Troilus and
Cressida,* and *All for Love,* the traditional stories are altered beyond recognition.

In *All for Love,* for instance, nonhistorical elements are not only
introduced as part of the plot but even constitute the mainsprings
of its action—Ventidius, a friend and mentor whose influence makes
Anthony lean toward duty; Dolabella, who loves Cleopatra and
provokes Anthony's jealousy which eventually causes him to stay
in Alexandria; Octavia and her children, and so forth. A plot
that is not well known makes it easier for an author to provoke

surprise, and surprise is the mainstay of the drama of intrigue. This serves Dryden's purpose but not Racine's.

In Racine, no element of surprise is derived from the plot. The simpler the plot and the better known, the more Racine relishes it. Where Corneille tries to focus the attention of the spectator on the act, Racine tries to eliminate the act per se in order to concentrate attention on the motive. The more audiences know of the plot, the less Racine has to tell them about it, and the freer he is to tackle other points of interest. With a familiar plot, there is no surprise or *coup de théâtre*, and the tension comes only from the interplay of human passions. As we know, this is not the case for Dryden's play. The range of the passions which he treats in them is so limited and repetitious that he could not afford the concentration of Racine. Dryden, like Corneille, needed the suspense and surprise derived from an unknown and crowded plot: one can read or view *The Conquest of Granada* over and over with nearly the same level of interest at each reading because it is practically impossible to remember the events in any logical order. The spectator is kept so busy trying to recall what happens that he has no time to reflect on why things happen. But as the plots of *Lear* or *Phèdre* or *Othello* become more familiar with each reading, these plays take on new dimensions, and the reader gains further insight into their meaning.

What has preceded is certainly no study of the comparative value of Corneille and Racine, and even less so of Dryden and Racine. The only validity of such a study, in relation to the heroic hero in Dryden's plays, is that it may throw some light on the nature of that hero. It has seemed interesting to show that within a certain literary tradition, in this case, neoclassicism, there can be not only divergence, but opposition in the nature of the works produced. This may be a truism. However, in the case of Dryden's plays, we have seen in the earlier part of this study how the majority of critics have always taken up form and matter as if they were interchangeable, concentrating mostly on form and making it responsible for the lack of interesting matter. That is, neoclassicism, with its profusion of critical tenets, was made answerable for the kind of play which Dryden and his contemporaries wrote and enjoyed. Dryden wrote the way he did because of the influence of the epic, the rule of the three unities, the concept of poetic justice, etc. To deny that these influences worked on Dryden is out of the question. But to assume that they were the shaping factors of his drama is to stretch the point too far. If, however, in my comparative analysis of the dramatic works of Dryden, Corneille, and Racine, I have succeeded in showing that, although working under the same critical influences, they nevertheless produced different kinds of drama, hopefully, this will represent a step forward in the understanding of Dryden's plays. The near identity between Dryden's and Corneille's concept of the drama takes on further importance when we stop to consider that Dryden was not only cognizant but also appreciative of the Elizabethan theatre and Shakespeare.

If, working within the same neoclassic tradition and doing their best to conform to its tenets, different dramatists arrive at different results, they must belong to different schools of thought. In other words, given one form, the only thing that can be different is the matter. Corneille's and Dryden's is one; Racine's, another. At one point in this study, I advanced the theory that the historical "moment" may have been a determining factor in the kind of drama which both Corneille and Dryden wrote. That Corneille's plays found renewed favor in the first half of the twentieth century was also mentioned. It is interesting to see how the historical "moment" theory applies in this case. It is impossible to go into each work and examine the validity of the arguments offered by critics in support of Corneille. A few facts, however may be sufficient to throw some light on the reasons for this trend. I have already pointed out that *Horace* was the play most frequently acted by the Comédie Française during World War I. Before the war Charles Péguy, the great Catholic poet, had already given impetus to a movement in favor of Corneille, a movement which stressed the sublime (*grandeur*), sacrifice, and transcendence of the self in Corneille's drama. Jean Schlumberger, in his *Plaisir à Corneille*, opposes Corneille's "art héroique" to Racine's "art de jouissance" and finds Corneille's art better suited to modern times; he is happy that with the growing appreciation of Corneille, he can see "l'austerité reprendre le pas sur l'hédonisme et la volonté sur l'intelligence." [30]

Robert Brasillach, in a long work extolling Corneille's greatness, compares him favorably with Shakespeare: "Oui, vraiment, il a été

notre Shakespeare." [31] Octave Nadal would explain the whole Cornelian world by the concept of "gloire." He believes that "passions,
sentiments, devoirs, vertus, sont tournés vers la gloire. Les conflits
qui peuvent naître entre eux, seule la gloire les résout." He differentiates "gloire" from "honneur," in that "gloire" is a personal obligation whereas "honneur" is obedience to rules: "Mais le sentiment
de la gloire, du moins dans son mouvement le plus beau, ressemble
plus à une exigence intime qu'à ce qu'on doit aux règles de l'honneur, toujours un peu extérieures." Nadal associates this "gloire"
with freedom: ". . . gloire secrète, qui répond à une exigence de la
nature profonde de l'homme cornélien et exprime en définitive sa
liberté intérieure." [32]

A most interesting critic is André Rousseaux, whose very per-
ceptiveness supplies the key to an understanding of the modern
movement in favor of Corneille.[33] Let us specify that Rousseaux's
favorable study on Corneille was written in 1941 during World
War II and was printed at that time in Canada. Rousseaux believes, like Schlumberger, that Corneille's characters are not torn
by conflict—"Ame sans problèmes"—and opposes them to Racine's,
who by concentrating on their inner motives display what Rousseaux calls "le culte du moi." He is of the opinion that *Horace* is
probably Corneille's most representative play because "cette espèce
d'héroisme absolue, où l'homme se réalise d'autant plus magnifique-
ment qu'il s'oublie davantage, convient tout à fait à la tendance de
Corneille, qui est de se détourner des problèmes pour s'évader
dans de beaux actes." [34] Rousseaux then, in spite of his use of the
word "évader," believes that Horace attains a fuller realization
by losing himself in the act he performs. When in another part
of his essay Rousseaux states that "l'élan verbal et l'élan moral ne
font qu'un dans la poésie cornélienne," he is being complimentary,
implying that the oral rhetoric necessarily means a moral reality.[35]
He goes further and advances the opinion that the first may produce the second: ". . . . est-il sûr même que le premier ne met pas
le second en mouvement?" [36]

Rousseaux is ready to admit that Corneille's drama is built on one
big heroic lie, "le mensonge héroïque," but he equates this lie with
charity: "le mensonge héroïque ou, si l'on veut, le jeu que l'homme
joue par vertu, par noblesse et générosité. C'est le jeu où une sorte
de charité parfois supérieure, parfois excessive, parfois même fantai-
siste, s'éxèrce aux dépens du jeu inverse, du jeu sévère et inexorable

de la vérité. . . . Le mensonge héroique est une forme du don de soi." [37] For Rousseaux, the Cornelian hero is a sort of Don Quixote. What makes Don Quixote great is that he believes in what he is fighting for, in an idea. Note the pessimism which Rousseaux unconsciously displays in the following passage:

> Or ce sont les idées qui demeurent, avec une pureté et une solidité inaltérables, au-dessus des objets que les atteintes du temps les incertitudes de notre perception, les illusions de notre sensibilité, les pauvres limites de notre intelligence rendent fragiles, caducs, douteux, vains souvent, et parfois sans existence réelle. Nous vivons parmi des moulins à vent et des mirages. Nous nous faisons de surprenantes images de la réalité des choses. Les arbres que nous croyons le plus fortement enracinés et dont nous admirons les cîmes moutonneuses, mais dont la nature chaque jour dévore la substance, n'ont peut-être pas une réalité beaucoup plus certaine que les nuages dont le vent fait et défait les architectures. Et cette chair même que notre âme anime, ces pieds qui nous portent, ce sang qui nous nourrit, et toute cette vie dont nous vivons et qui nous continuera, que d'illusions en elle, qui s'y renouvellent, y foisonnent y font étendue et volume! Le mensonge est le tissu de la vie terrestre. [38]

In a later essay Rousseaux stresses the predominance of sacrifice in Corneille's plays. This opinion is hard to understand. Where does sacrifice reside for Horace when all he feels is exhilaration and fulfillment as the results of his act? The logic of the happy ending denies all sacrificial value to any act, on these grounds, by the hero. On the other hand, Rousseaux defends Corneille against any accusation that he is an exponent of authority and strength. If the state or the king are magnified to such a great extent in Corneille, Rousseaux believes that it is because the state or the King represents all individuals and can ask of them, on these premises, any sacrifice it deems necessary. It is difficult to understand how, as Rousseaux wrote this second essay after the war, he could not see how close he was to totalitarian ideology:

> Il montre dans le souverain selon Corneille un homme dont la *gloire* peut exiger de tous les autres humains ce que, chez le héros cornélien qui n'est pas roi, la *gloire* exige de lui seul. Chez le roi cornélien, le mécanisme sacrificiel dont la *gloire* est le moteur se transpose de la vie personnelle à toute la société humaine. [39]

If we have dwelt at some length on Rousseaux, it is because we find him representative. His stand and that of the other critics mentioned seem to reflect the growing feeling of insecurity in the twentieth century—the need, in troubled times, for action that promises results, for the dubious security that is linked with order and conformity. In other words, our historical "moment" has much in common with the historical "moment" in which Corneille wrote in the 1630's and Dryden in the 1670's.

NOTES

CHAPTER 1

1   Lewis N. Chase, *The English Heroic Play* (New York, 1903), 46, 52, 111.
2   J. W. Tupper, "The Relation of the Heroic Play to the Romances of Beaumont and Fletcher," *PMLA*, XX (1905), 602.
3   Margaret Sherwood, *Dryden's Dramatic Theory and Practice* (New Haven, 1914), 66.
4   B. J. Pendlebury, *Dryden's Heroic Plays: A Study of the Origin* (London, 1923), 8.
5   Allardyce Nicoll, *British Drama* (London, 1925), 225.
6   Bonamy Dobrée, *Restoration Tragedy, 1660–1720* (Oxford, 1929), 33, and *John Dryden* (London, 1956).
7   Chase, *English Heroic Play*, 107.
8   *Ibid.*, 194.
9   Pendlebury, *Dryden's Heroic Plays*, 8.
10 Davenant's *The Siege of Rhodes* was first acted in 1656.
11 *Works of Dryden*, ed. Sir Walter Scott and George Saintsbury (18 vols.; Edinburgh, 1882–93), II, 317.
12 A. W. Ward, *A History of English Dramatic Literature to the Death of Queen Anne* (2nd ed., 3 vols.; London, 1899), III, 301.
13 Chase, *English Heroic Play*, 22.
14 C. G. Child, "The Rise of the Heroic Play," *MLN*, XIX (1904), 168.
15 *Ibid.*, 168–69.
16 Tupper, "Relation of Heroic Play to Beaumont and Fletcher," 587.
17 Sherwood, *Dryden's Dramatic Theory*, 60.
18 F. E. Schelling, *English Drama* (New York, 1914), 182.
19 *Ibid.*, 244.
20 Pendlebury, *Dryden's Heroic Plays*, 6.
21 *Ibid.*, 8.
22 *Ibid.*, 9.
23 Allardyce Nicoll, *A History of Restoration Drama, 1660–1700* (Cambridge, 1928), 82.

24 W. S. Clark, "The Sources of the Restoration Heroic Play," *RES*, IV (1928), 63.
25 Dobrée, *Restoration Tragedy*, 27.
26 *Ibid.*, 16.
27 Nicoll, *Restoration Drama*, 79.
28 Dobrée, *John Dryden*, 17–18.
29 Kathleen Lynch, "Conventions of Platonic Drama in the Heroic Plays of Orrery and Dryden," *PMLA*, XLIV (1929), 457.
30 *Ibid.*
31 *Ibid.*, 458.
32 S. C. Osborn, "Heroical Love in Dryden's Heroic Drama," *PMLA*, LXXIII (1958), 481.
33 *Ibid.*, 484.
34 *Ibid.*, 487.
35 Mildred E. Hartsock, "Dryden's Plays: A Study in Ideas," in *Seventeenth Century Studies*, 2nd Series, ed. Robert Shafer (Princeton, 1937), 74.
36 *Ibid.*, 89.
37 *Ibid.*, 174.
38 J. A. Winterbottom, "The Place of Hobbesian Ideas in Dryden's Tragedies," *JEGP*, LXVII (1948), 665–83. In a preceding article, "The Development of the Hero in Dryden's Plays," *JEGP*, LII (1953), 161–73, Winterbottom develops the theory that in the later plays the hero is more social than in the earlier plays, but on the whole he seems to accept the conventional portrait of the heroic hero as a ranting self-centered individual.
39 A. E. Parsons, "The English Heroic Play," *MLR*, XXII (1938), 3.
40 *Ibid.*, 6.
41 Cecil V. Deane, *Dramatic Theory and the Rhymed Heroic Play* (London, 1931).
42 David Nichol Smith, *John Dryden* (Cambridge, 1950), 32.
43 Thomas H. Fujimura, "The Appeal of Dryden's Heroic Plays," *PMLA*, LXXV (1960), 37.
44 *Ibid.*, 34.
45 *Ibid.*, 37, 40.
46 *Ibid.*, 42.
47 *Ibid.*, 47.
48 Jean Gagen, "Love and Honor in Dryden's Heroic Plays," *PMLA*, LXXVII (1962), 209.
49 Curtis Watson, *Shakespeare and the Renaissance Concept of Honor* (Princeton, 1960).
50 Gagen, "Love and Honor in Dryden," 219.
51 Cyrus Hoy, "The Effect of the Restoration on the Drama," *TSL*, VI (1961), 87.
52 *Ibid.*, 88.
53 *Ibid.*, 89.
54 *Ibid.*
55 *Ibid.*, 91.

CHAPTER 2

1 *Dryden*, ed. George Saintsbury (New York, n.d.), xiv.
2 *Dryden: The Dramatic Works*, ed. Montague Summers (6 vols.; London,

1931–1932), II, 331. This work will hereinafter be cited as *Dramatic Works.*

CHAPTER 3

1 Chase, *English Heroic Play,* 117, 121.
2 *Ibid.,* 192.
3 Tupper, "Relation of Heroic Play to Beaumont and Fletcher," 585.
4 *Ibid.,* 617.
5 Sherwood, *Dryden's Dramatic Theory,* 62.
6 Tupper, "Relation of Heroic Play to Beaumont and Fletcher," 616.
7 Hartsock, "Dryden's Plays," 120, 117, 116.
8 Dobrée, *Restoration Tragedy,* 22.
9 Dobrée, *Dryden,* 18.
10 *Ibid.,* 25.
11 *Cf.* Jean Gagen, "Love and Honor in Dryden's Heroic Plays"; Curtis Watson, *Shakespeare and the Renaissance Concept of Honor;* also C. L. Barber, *The Idea of Honour in English Drama—1591–1700* (Götebord, Sweden, 1957).
12 Tupper, "Relation of Heroic Play to Beaumont and Fletcher," 594.
13 Sherwood, *Dryden's Dramatic Theory,* 61.
14 Tupper, "Relation of Heroic Play to Tupper and Fletcher," 585.
15 Pendlebury, *Dryden's Heroic Plays,* 25.
16 *Ibid.,* 110.
17 M. W. Alssid, "Dryden's Rhymed Heroic Tragedies: A Critical Study of the Plays and Their Place in Dryden's Poetry," *DA,* XX, 3281.
18 *Dramatic Works,* II, 331.
19 Hartsock, "Dryden's Plays," 125.
20 Fujimura, "Appeal of Dryden's Heroic Plays," 39.
21 *Ibid.,* 42.
22 *Ibid.*
23 Gagen, "Love and Honor in Dryden," 209.
24 Fujimura, "Appeal of Dryden's Heroic Plays," 40.
25 Dobrée, *Restoration Tragedy,* 94. Dobrée is only one of many critics who hold this point of view; *e.g.,* Margaret Sherwood, *Dryden's Dramatic Theory and Practice,* 12: "Dryden . . . has left an art, tentative, uncertain, held together neither by deep intellectual conviction nor by unconscious instinct, but showing a lack of controlling idea, a tendency to fall apart."
26 Tupper, "Relation of Heroic Play to Beaumont and Fletcher," 602.
27 *Essays of John Dryden,* ed. W. P. Ker (2 vols.; London, 1900), II, 127–28. This work is hereinafter referred to as *Essays.*
28 *Ibid.,* I, 213.
29 Pendlebury, *Dryden's Heroic Plays,* 115.
30 *Ibid.,* 102.
31 Sherwood, *Dryden's Dramatic Theory,* 12.
32 Alssid, for instance (in his unpublished dissertation, already mentioned), concentrates on Dryden's "Of Heroic Plays."

CHAPTER 4

1 Ernst Cassirer, *The Mind of the Enlightenment,* trans. Fritz C. A. Loelln and James P. Pettegrove (Princeton, 1951).
2 Paul Hazard, *La Crise de la Conscience Européenne* (3 vols.; Paris, 1935).

3   *Ibid.*, I, iv.

4   Terms are often misinterpreted. The "individual" here is, of course, given its classical connotation of "typical" or "universal," and is not the personal individual of romanticism.

5   Francis Galloway, *Reason, Rule and Revolt in English Classicism* (New York, 1940), 21.

6   *Dramatic Works,* II, 330.

7   Samuel H. Monk, *The Sublime in Eighteenth Century England* (New York, 1935), 10–42.

8   *The Great Critics,* ed. James Harry Smith and Edd Winfield Parks (New York, 1932), 70–72.

9   Hazard, *Crise de la Conscience Européenne,* I, 175.

10 *Essays,* II, 171.

11 Katherine E. Wheatley, *Racine and English Classicism* (Austin, 1956), 234.

12 Louis I. Bredvold, *The Intellectual Milieu of John Dryden* (Ann Arbor, 1934).

13 *Ibid.,* 15.

14 *Ibid.,* 71.

15 *Ibid.,* 85.

16 *Ibid.,* 115.

17 *Ibid.,* 128.

18 *Ibid.,* 136.

19 *Ibid.,* 147.

20 *Ibid.,* 132.

21 *Cf.* E. Vernon Arnold, *Roman Stoicism* (Cambridge, 1911) on the interrelation of Stoicism and Christianity, 408–36.

22 J. A. Winterbottom, "Stoicism in Dryden's Tragedies," *JEGP,* LXI, (1962), 872.

23 *Ibid.,* 873.

24 *Cf.* Marvin T. Herrick, *The Fusion of Horatian and Aristotelian Literary Criticism, 1531–1555,* "Illinois Studies in Language and Literature," XXXII (Urbana, 1934); Clarence C. Green, *The Neo-Classic Theory in England during the Eighteenth Century* (Cambridge, Mass., 1934); C. F. Deane, *Dramatic Theory and the Rhymed Heroic Play,* already cited; J. W. H. Atkins, *English Literary Criticism: Seventeenth and Eighteenth Centuries* (London, 1951), 7–12.

25 *Essays,* II, 125, 126, 143.

26 *Ibid.,* 125.

27 Winterbottom, "Stoicism in Dryden's Tragedies," 882.

28 *Ibid.*

29 *Ibid.,* 883.

30 *Ibid.*

31 Edwyn Bevan, *Stoics and Sceptics* (Oxford, 1913), 33, 34, 32, 44.

32 R. M. Wenley, *Stoicism and Its Influences* (New York, 1927), 75.

33 *Ibid.,* 99.

34 *Essays,* II, 177. Dryden is speaking here of an epic hero, referring especially to Aeneas, but we know that he considered tragedy and epic as closely related genres.

35 Fujimura, "Appeal of Dryden's Heroic Plays," 48, 40.

CHAPTER 5

1   Alan D. McKillop, *English Literature from Dryden to Burns* (New York,

1948). One, of course, does not turn to manuals or anthologies for the best in literary criticism. But such works are very useful to the extent that they usually represent the most commonly adopted point of view, reflecting a certain "stratification" of critical outlook which is sometimes very hard to shake off.

2 Pendlebury, *Dryden's Heroic Plays*, 125.

3 G. H. Nettleton, *English Drama of the Restoration and Eighteenth Century, 1642–1780* (New York, 1923), 68.

4 Deane, *Dramatic Theory and the Rhymed Heroic Play*, 180–83.

5 *Cf.* Marvin T. Herrick, *Tragicomedy, Its Origin and Development in Italy, France and England*, "Illinois Studies in Language and Literature," XXXIX (Urbana, 1955), on the different meanings and concepts attached at various periods to the term tragicomedy.

6 *Dramatic Works, IV*, 188–262.

7 It seemed preferable to discuss Shakespeare's Lear rather than his Antony. A comparison of the two Antonies would have added a third dimension which would only have been a source of confusion. At any rate, this discussion is not about the character of Antony per se, but about the hero in Dryden's plays as opposed to the Shakespearean hero.

8 *Dramatic Works, IV,* 180.

9 *Essays,* II, 126.

10 *Dramatic Works,* III, 164.

11 Dobrée, *Dryden,* 275.

12 *The Critical Works of Thomas Rymer*, ed. Curt A. Zimansky (New Haven, 1956), 132. Katherine Wheatley believes he is serious; Louis Charlanne in *L'Influence Française au XVIIᵉ Siècle* (Paris, 1906), 576, is sure that the morals which Rymer offers are in jest, and he is probably right since throughout this piece of criticism, Rymer is intent on ridiculing Shakespeare.

13 Rymer, *Critical Works,* 132, 134.

14 *Ibid.,* 135.

15 *Ibid.,* 161.

16 *Dramatic Works,* IV, 181.

17 *Dramatic Works,* V, 127–201.

18 *Ibid.,* VI, 335–97.

19 *Ibid,* 29–132.

20 *Ibid.,* IV, 354–426.

CHAPTER 6

1 *Cf. Essays of John Dryden*, ed. W. P. Ker, Vol. I, where Ker stresses this point throughout his introduction; also Pierre Legouis, "Corneille and Dryden as Dramatic Critics," *Seventeenth Century Studies* (Oxford, 1938), 269–91; and Arthur C. Kirsch, "Dryden, Corneille and the Heroic Play," *ELH*, LIX (1962), 248–64.

2 *Oeuvres de Pierre Corneille*, ed. Charles Joseph Marty-Laveaux (12 vols.; Paris, 1910–1922), I, 13–122.

3 *Ibid.,* 14.

4 *Ibid.,* 16.

5 *Ibid.,* 17.

6 *Ibid.,* 21.

7 *Ibid.*

8 *Ibid.,* 57.

9 *Ibid.*

10   *Ibid.,* 53.
11   *Ibid.,* 57–58.
12   *Ibid.,* 58.
13   *Ibid.,* 63.
14   *Ibid.,* 68–69.
15   *Ibid.*
16   *Ibid.,* 58.
17   *Ibid.,* 79–80.
18   *Ibid.,* III 282–358.
19   Cited *ibid.,* III, 256.
20   *Ibid.,* 273.
21   *Ibid.,* 275.
22   *Ibid.* Corneille is alluding to Horace's trial in Act V for the murder of Camille where he is only saved by his father's plea and in consideration of his past services to his country.
23   *Oeuvres de J. Racine,* ed. Paul Mesnard (2nd. ed., 8 vols.; Paris, 1921–1925), II, 375.
24   *Ibid.,* II, 376.
25   *Ibid.,* 382–454.
26   Georges May, *Tragédie Cornélienne, Tragédie Racinienne,* "Illinois Studies in Language and Literature," XXXII (Urbana, 1948), 13.
27   *Ibid.,* 14.
28   *Ibid.,* 21.
29   *Ibid.,* 25.
30   Jean Schlumberger, *Plaisir à Corneille* (Paris, 1936), 10.
31   Robert Brasillach, *Pierre Corneille* (Paris, 1938), 373. A fact that may be of interest is that Brasillach was noted for his collaboration with the Nazi regime during World War II.
32   Octave Nadal, *Le sentiment de l'amour dans l'oeuvre de Pierre Corneille* (Paris, 1948), 302, 299, 307.
33   André Rousseaux, *Le Monde Classique* (4 vols.; Paris, 1941–1956).
34   *Ibid.,* 47–48.
35   *Ibid.,* 51.
36   *Ibid.*
37   *Ibid,* 56.
38   *Ibid.,* 63–64.
39   Rousseaux, *Le Monde Classique,* III, 149.

INDEX

LOUISIANA STATE UNIVERSITY STUDIES

The Studies was established to publish the results of research by faculty members, staff, and graduate students of the University. Manuscripts of exceptional merit from sources other than aforementioned are considered for publication provided they deal with subjects of particular interest to Louisiana.

The Studies originally appeared as a unified series consisting of forty-two numbers, published between the years 1931 and 1941. In 1951 the Studies was reactivated, and is now being issued in the following series: Social Sciences, Humanities, Biological Sciences, Physical Sciences, and Coastal Studies. Other series may be established as the need arises.